PARENTING WITH PETS

THE MAGIC OF RAISING CHILDREN WITH ANIMALS

CHRISTINE HAMER & MARGARET HEVEL

BOOK PUBLISHERS NETWORK

Book Publishers Network
P.O. Box 2256
Bothell • WA • 98041
PH • 425-483-3040

10 9 8 7 6 5 4 3 2

Printed in the United States of America

LCCN: 2007935342
ISBN10: 1-887542-58-2
ISBN 13: 978-1-887542-58-6

Proofreader: Julie Scandora
Cover Design: Laura Zugzda
Interior Layout: Stephanie Martindale

Dedication

To all the pets who have enriched our lives and made us better parents.

Contents

Acknowledgements

This book was created as a dedication of our love for animals and children. We have been enriched because of their involvement in our lives. Several stories in the book were written by children; we thank them for sharing. We also have many adults to thank for their contributions. Molly and Bonnie, your stories were great. A special thank you to Gail Hanninen for collecting so many of the children's stories, Liz Wilson and Pam Bennett for reviewing the sections on parrots and cats, and the many readers who gave us valuable feedback and helped to improve the book.

We also wish to thank our family and friends for all their support and for reading versions of the book as it evolved. Last but certainly not the least; we would like to thank you, dear reader for buying our book.

WHY THIS MATTERS

Nothing's impossible in my world of make-believe.
Birds move in the air above. Some day I'll join them.
I can fly to the ground from huge rocks and big logs.
And . . .once I flew from the top board fence . . .
That's a long ways.
Wanna see?

-Margaret Hevel

Ask children about their animal friends and watch their faces light up. Animals touch an intimate part of our souls and enrich our lives. They can be a working partner or a guardian angel. Even the most jaded adolescent will soften when shown the furry faces of kittens or puppies. Animals ground us. They help us not to take ourselves too seriously. Their very nature impels us to earn their trust. Their unwavering faith in us invites us to live at our best.

This sense of well-being and of being loved should be reason enough to recommend that all families include animals in their lives. However, there are also physiological benefits to owning a pet.

These health benefits are even gaining attention from the medical community. As a key seminar speaker in 2002, Doctor Edward Creagan, a Mayo Clinic cancer specialist said, "I consider getting a pet to be one of the easiest and most rewarding ways to living a longer, healthier life."

In Canada, the government is considering a bill that would subsidize the costs of pet ownership for the elderly. Supporters of this bill claim that the money spent on pet welfare will be offset by a reduction in medical and health care expenses. Their claims are based on some substantial studies. In 1999, Petnet Australia estimated that companion animals saved the Australian government a whopping 2.27 billion dollars of health care expenditures. The study found that when compared to non-pet owners, people who own pets visit the doctor less often, use less medication, have lower cholesterol and blood pressure, recover more quickly from illness and surgery, are less lonely, and deal better with stress.

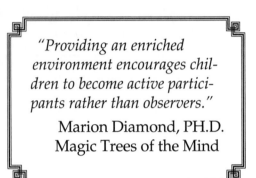

"Providing an enriched environment encourages children to become active participants rather than observers."

Marion Diamond, PH.D.
Magic Trees of the Mind

The elderly are not the only ones plagued by stress. Stresses placed on our children have skyrocketed over the past twenty years. Children as young as nine years old are experiencing panic attacks, and twelve-year-olds are suffering from ulcers. Chronic stress can elevate blood pressure, a major cause of cardiovascular disease. Some elementary schools, aware of the growing epidemic, are offering stress-reduction classes.

Adolescence is one of the most stressful times in human growth and development. Not only is society placing pressure on youth, but also the adolescent's body is changing at a rapid rate. Teen suicide and homicide rates have tripled. Teens have so much going on in their lives that, as parents, we often walk that fine line between encouragement and intrusion. Teaching teens methods to handle stress can help reduce their anxiety. For instance, encouraging a teen to take the dog on regular walks can be very therapeutic, both physically and emotionally. During physical activity, the body stimulates the release of hormones that combat depression. Walking with a dog will take advantage of the pet's natural calming effect in addition to the benefits of walking.

In February of 2000, researchers at State University of New York in Buffalo studied a group of stockbrokers, one of the most stressful professions. As part of the research, the stockbrokers were paired with a pet in order to study the effects of having a pet in the family. Although all of the subjects showed some kind of health issues at the start of the research, the results showed that a pet provided a positive impact on the general health and well-being of the stockbrokers. The researchers admitted they were not sure exactly how the animals effected the positive changes. They hypothesized, however, that it had to do with reliability and consistency. They believe that pets provide a calming comfort in an otherwise chaotic world. A companion pet can offer this same comfort and consistency to our children.

Another reason a companion pet's presence can be so important for our children is its effect as an antidepressant. One study found that a few minutes of cuddling a pet relieved more stress than talking with a parent or a friend. Further, if a child is carrying out an unpleasant task such as a dreaded homework assignment, a pet's presences was more effective in making the task palatable than having a human companion.

At Purdue University Center for the Human-Animals Bond, Dr. Alan Beck found that nearly seventy percent of children confide in their pets. The children said that they knew their pets would not betray them or their secrets. In general, children gave animals high scores for listening, reassurance, appreciation, and companionship. They also believed their pets provided them with unconditional love. One 1985 Michigan study found that seventy-five percent of children age ten to fourteen turned to their feathered or furry friend when they felt upset. Pets don't discriminate and they don't judge.

A pet can serve as a safe outlet for different family members to share with one another. Pets offer parents teachable moments; they can be a conduit both for our children's and for our emotions.

Communication that might be stilted and difficult can flow smoothly over the shared task of grooming a pet or cleaning a cage.

A pet's ability to open communication is especially important for teens who are more apt to bury their feelings than to express them. Adolescents are often so confused that it may be impossible for them to find the right words to convey what they are feeling. If children loose the ability to talk about their feelings, they may become depressed and therefore feel alienated and alone. Animals can help teens through this difficult time because they demand interaction. The attention needed from the teen may be as simple as tending to the animal's basic needs or as complex as giving a training session.

Animals respond to sunrises and sunsets, to the pulse of seasons, to the gravitational pull caused by the changing phases of the moon. By spending time with animals, we relax, our pulse slows, our pace tempers. We reconnect to a natural sense of time long forgotten. Let us take you on a journey to explore the value of letting  pets and nature into your home. We feel the gifts that animals and nature bring will enrich your lives. They will provide you with varied opportunities for teaching and for creating gateways to communicating with your children. Some of the activities we suggest cost as little as a pencil and piece of paper. Others can be more involved.

As you read through this book, we invite you to listen, talk, and become involved in the life of your child. There is only one key ingredient to successful parenting: time. We must touch the lives of our children daily, or one day we may realize that our children are grown and gone and our chance to influence their lives has passed. The best parenting costs nothing...love is free.

CHILDREN AND PETS

"A child who is exposed to the emotional experiences inherent in playing with a pet is given many learning opportunities that are essential to wholesome personality development"
-Boris Levinson
Child psychologist

"Mommy, Daddy, can I *pleeeease* get him? I promise I'll take care of him all on my own." Most parents at one time or another have been subjected to the persistent pleas of a child whose heart has been captured by a creature of nature. Usually it is the cuddly furriness of a puppy or kitten.

As tempting as it is to give in, the decision to add a new life to the family should not be an impulsive one. As parents, we teach by example. Our preparation for and careful consideration of adding a new family member is the first step in parenting with a pet. This important beginning models responsibility to our child at its most basic level. When we control the buying impulse, we teach our children to stop and think before they act. It is important for parents to remember the difference between the purchases of inanimate objects, such as toys, and the commitment to another living creature. A pet should not be seen as disposable.

Why Get a Pet and What to Expect

There is evidence that the presence of animals can alter children's attitudes toward themselves and their ability to relate to others. Live animals are catalysts for social and verbal interactions among children. According to one study, animals as varied as dogs, birds, and spiders facilitated social interactions.

Brenda Bryant, a University of California-Davis Applied Behavioral Science Professor, explains that experiences with pets increase competence in children in ways that other learned tasks cannot. In addition to increased verbal skills, children naturally become more attuned to nonverbal communication as a result of interactions with their pet. This comes from their practice at "reading" their pet's body language. But this skill is not restricted to their pet. These children also demonstrated the ability to draw the correct conclusions about emotions from human faces more accurately than those from homes without a pet.

Students with a companion animal are able to express their emotions more freely than children from homes without a pet. This may be due in part to the nonjudgmental attitude of animals. These children also had an easier time in social situations and were more adept at problem solving.

As the child grows, his or her world becomes more and more complex and stressful. A pet in the family can provide a child with a constant. This security allows the child to experiment with different strategies to reduce stress. As parents, we can help coach our children with positive means for them to handle their daily pressures both at home and at school.

Sarah stomped through the front door, slammed her backpack on the floor, slumped into the kitchen chair, and heaved a huge sigh.

"I can see you've had a hard day."

Sarah glared at her mother and rolled her eyes.

"You know, Daisy has been sitting at the gate all afternoon waiting for you to get home and take her for a walk."

"I don't feel like it right now," Sarah mumbled.

"I know you don't; I can tell how upset you are. However, it's really important that Daisy get out for her walk. I'll have a snack ready for you when you get back." Her mother put an arm around her daughter's shoulder. "If you feel like talking, I'll listen."

Sarah heaved a sigh and grabbed Daisy's leash.

"Sarah?"

She turned and scowled at her mother.

"You know I love you?" her mother said.

"Yeah, I know."

Sarah walked into the backyard and sat down on the step. Daisy wiggled over to the teen and tucked a nose under her hand. Her soft brown eyes watched Sarah. Almost absentmindedly, Sarah stroked Daisy's fur. With each even stroke, Sarah relaxed. Daisy sat beside Sarah, enjoying the attention. After a while, Sarah smiled at her companion. "OK, ready for your walk?" Daisy danced around Sarah eager for the adventure she knew was attached to those words. Sarah laughed at the antics of her excited pup then snapped on the leash. As they started down the front walk, Sarah was sharing Daisy's happiness and had all but forgotten the upset that had caused her to feel angry.

Most of the time a pet is eagerly accepted into the home. Occasionally, however, the idea of having a pet is more attractive than the real thing. Some children, especially toddlers, may find the new family member frightening. This reaction is not unusual and resembles the response that youngsters might display when a new sibling becomes part of the family. It is important for young children to feel secure with the new relationship and for them to understand that this new addition is not a threat to their being loved. Parents can help with this transition by displaying excitement about the new family member. This will help the fearful child see that there is no cause for alarm.

When the pet first arrives home, everyone will be excited to hold and interact with the new family member, but they may find the animal's sudden movements upsetting. As parents we can reduce this fear by creating a safe environment for both the child and the pet as they become acquainted. Since all animals need time to adjust to their new surroundings, we can explain the need to keep a quiet voice and to move slowly. This becomes a wonderful opportunity for us to explain about considering someone else's feelings. By asking our children to consider how frightening this experience must be for their pet, we exemplify empathy and sensitivity. In addition, a relaxed animal is more likely to respond in a positive fashion to the child's overtures.

Older children may lose interest after finally getting the longed-for pet. According to Dr. Marty Becker in his book, *Healing Power of Pets*, around ninety-nine percent of children say that they want a pet. That doesn't mean, however, that ninety-nine percent of children want the secondary, unpleasant tasks of picking up dog poop, changing the litter box, or cleaning a bird or rodent cage. However, in order for children to gain the full benefits associated with animals, they must do these chores. Caring for the needs of an animal allows a child to give something the animal cannot attain on its own. By providing their animal with food, water, and clean housing, children discover that they are needed and relied upon in a way they most likely have not experienced before. Responsibility is a natural outcome of the realization that, in this world, each person is necessary and uniquely important.

As is true with anything in life, children learn that the more they put into their relationship with their pet, the more they will get in return. Many parents believe that the love from their family pet is as emotionally supportive as the love provided by other family members. For a child to reap the most benefit from the companion-animal experience, there must be a relationship between the two. With this in mind, those animals that more naturally interact with and elicit a caring response from the child will be the most effective pets. Although some children may feel affection toward amphibians or reptiles, most humans naturally gravitate to those animals with the "cuddle factor."

With our guidance, children learn that, although different animals need to be handled in different ways, all pets, whether of fur, fin, or feather, must be treated with kindness and respect. Although a child may be sweet and loving, he or she will not know instinctively the proper way to handle the new non-human friend. As parents, an element of the undertaking we accept when we adopted a family pet is the responsibility of keeping both the pet and the child safe. This includes both physical and mental safety. Part of our purpose in adding a pet to our family is to involve our children in the joyous connection that animals can provide. This experience will not be enjoyable, however, if we don't take the time to start the relationship between all family members on a positive note. Children, who learn to care for an animal with kindness and patience, learn invaluable lessons in how to treat people as well.

Parents should serve as role models. A family pet gives parents a chance to demonstrate the proper care and feeding of an animal and, more important, the opportunity to show how to love and give praise. Witnessing and participating in this healthy relationship can help children with the development of nonverbal communication, of compassion, and of empathy.

There will be frustrating times with the addition of a pet. However, if a parent is willing to continue working to build a relationship, the advantages of having a pet far outweigh the irritating moments. Many times these upsets are marvelous teaching opportunities if we only take the time to look at the situation.

THE ROLE OF A PET IN THE CHANGING CHILD

I am a part of all that I have met.

\- Alfred Tennyson

A Legacy of Love

As a very young girl, I knew I was connected in some special way to animals. I didn't have the words to express this, only my feelings inside. My curiosity took me into meadows and woods. I explored the habitats of other living creatures along the waters of ponds, rivers, and lakes. I made pets of pollywogs and watched them become frogs. I marveled at caterpillars that blossomed into butterflies. My canary and my rabbit lived in harmony with my cat. And, always, my special buddy in play was my dog. I firmly believe that these lovely and diverse creatures helped to provide a center, a grounding that was my well to draw from and a place to nurture my spirit when life threw me out of balance.

My husband and I were fortunate to raise our four daughters on a small Montana ranch. Our animal family included chickens, cattle, a couple of horses, rabbits, a milk cow, two milking goats, a kitty, and two family dogs.

These animals gave my daughters the same sense of wonder and self-discovery that I experienced as a girl. They were a vessel to hold sorrows and gave warmth when the world seemed cold and uncaring. They were a constant when life was changing faster than the young women could understand.

My daughters are now grown women with families of their own. My husband and I have the privilege of watching our grandchildren absorb the same benefits from their connection to their own pets.

Perhaps this legacy of love is as important a reason as any for inviting companion animals into our home.

- Margaret Hevel

Home, Our Childhood Center

Home is a child's center during his or her growth and development years. It should be an environment where unconditional love can foster a sense of self-worth. The world is complex. Learning to balance these complexities while maintaining a sense of inner peace is a lifelong skill. Born in childhood, these embryonic resources can be nurtured by the skillful guidance of parents and aided by family pets. At the CAIRC (Companion Animal Information & Research Center) symposium, speakers addressed the significant relationship between pets and children. One of the topics discussed was the impact that computers and an urban lifestyle have had on the development of modern children. Both, they concluded, tended to isolate children from the natural world, thereby promoting selfish behavior because it removed the child from a sense of responsibility for the world around them. One mitigating measure that they discussed was the influence of pets on the emotional and spiritual growth of our children.

A child's emotional balance can be restored with the calming effects of an animal. To look into a dog's loving eyes, to feel the warmth and constant rhythm of a horse, to giggle at the antics of a kitten or a hamster, or to wonder about the movement of goldfish all bring moments of pure joy.

Over 125 years ago in his book, Horseback Riding, A Medical Point of View, Dr. Ghislani Durant wrote about the therapeutic benefits of horses. That physical and mental benefit of riding described so long ago is being revisited today.

As a NARHA (North America Riding for the Handicapped Association) Certified Instructor in the equine therapeutic program in Salmon, Idaho, I've seen the physical and mental benefits horses can provide both children and young adults. It is always a personal thrill to watch nurturing bonds develop between horse and rider.

Working with instructors and their equine partners, developmentally and emotionally challenged children have shown improvements in coordination, muscular strength, posture, balance, motivation, and self-esteem.

The equine vaulting program was one such program designed to promote self-esteem for "at risk" youth. The teens began the program by walking with their equine partner, mimicking the same rhythm and leg movement of the horse. At first these young people were scared, nervous, or angry. Often they shielded their true nature with plastic attitudes of "prove it" or "I could care less." As the partnership between the teen and the animal developed, the pair would trot and then run in synchronicity. The duo graduated to games designed to promote and deepen the bond between horse and child. Besides aerobic exercise, these young people experienced enhanced motor skills, body awareness, spatial orientation, rhythm, and concentration.

For these young people trust is at risk. The fragile acceptance of horse and rider grew during gentle relaxation exercises they practiced on horseback, during grooming, and in care-giving. The children observed and assisted their teammates during vaulting classes. They learned patience, positive social skills, and teamwork. During the course, both parents and teachers witnessed positive changes in attitude and in classroom participation.

On graduation day, the teens put on a performance for parents, teachers, and friends. One single parent, sitting in the bleachers, began to cry. Through tears, she confided in me. "I've never seen my son perform until today. He's always been in trouble everywhere else. It's nice to see him smile."

Another youth was at a stalemate in her therapy program. After the vaulting training, there was a breakthrough in her sessions. Both the counselor and the girl contribute the progress she made to the bond that she developed with her horse during the vaulting program.

As young children, these troubled teens learned to stand, to walk, and to run for no one but himself or herself. As young adults, they learn to walk, trot, and run in a partnership with their horse and their teammates. Through this harmony, they gained the confidence and the courage to reach out and change their life in positive ways.

- Margaret Hevel

The Developmental Years

Studies suggest that animal companions aid in the development of nurturing behavior and humane attitudes in children and can help socialization of young adults and their peers.

- Allen Schoen
Kindred Spirits

Let's examine how pets can be an integral part of the growth and development for preschool, elementary, junior high, and high school children.

Preschool

All children learn the same basic skills like walking and talking, or learning to eat on their own. But, they do not necessarily learn these skills at the same time. Heredity, nutrition, and health can influence skill development. Other aspects that can influence a child's development are environmental factors and social enrichment.

Petting and grooming animals can provide the tactile stimulation that is so important during early toddler development. This interaction can also open opportunities for language development. "Feel how soft puppy's fur is? Where are puppy's eyes? Where are your eyes? Where are mommy's eyes?"

Children watch their parents for clues about what to do and about how to react to different social interactions. In *New Perspectives on Our Lives with Companion Animals*, the authors, A. Katcher and A.M. Beck, mention how important it is for parents to demonstrate how to praise, how to touch gently, and how to speak softly to their pet. Besides being beneficial to the relationship between child and pet, this is also a wonderful way to teach children the social skills that are needed for a positive relationship with human playmates. Thus as parents, we have significant influences in shaping our children's behaviors through positive modeling.

Ruth had just finished her lunch and, like most toddlers learning to feed themselves, had sticky hands and food everywhere. Her mother approached her with a wet rag to clean up the mess. Ruth threw her arms in front of her face. "No, no, no!" she screamed. Ruth's mother took a step back from the highchair and waited for Ruth to calm down. Curious, Ruth peeked out between her fingers. "Look at your kitty, Smokey," Mother said. Ruth looked at the cat sitting on the floor grooming his face. "He knows how important it is to clean up after his meal. I think that we should clean up too. Why don't you wash your face like Smokey, and then I'll just find the little bits that you might have missed." Ruth smiled and took the cloth from her mother.

Children will often take the parent's role when interacting with their pet and "teach" their own learned behaviors to the animal. This play also provides practice of the newly acquired skill through repetition.

The next day Ruth was playing with her favorite doll. She took the bottom of her shirt to wipe across her doll's face. Ruth pulled her doll away and shook the doll's head side to side. "It's okay, dolly," she soothed. Ruth then put her shirt bottom in the doll's hand, and together they wiped the doll's face. "All clean now!"

Therefore, our behavior toward our children, toward other people and toward our pets will have direct impact on the kind of social play our children practice.

As parents, we can encourage our child to explore his or her environment by modeling an interest in the world around us. Asking questions, such as "See how the fish wiggles his body? Why do you think he does that? Can you wiggle like a fish?" can help engage a child in the curiosity of nature. When a child identifies with nature or a pet, parents have the opportunity to point out the similarities and differences between the child and the rest of the animal kingdom. This simple conversation is educational and teaches body awareness.

Children relate to animals and will often dream about them. Therefore, using stories about animals can have direct meaning for the child and can serve as a great method for teaching children morals and other important lessons.

I still recall my mother retelling McGuffey *animal stories from her youth. These books, filled with life lessons, had become patched and dog-eared, handed down from one generation to the next. In a one-room schoolhouse with a potbelly stove, my grandmother was introduced to* The McGuffey Readers. *The beginning series were stories about a farmer and his animals. They were designed to teach morality in a friendly, simple way. Each story ended with a lesson in handling a life situation in a successful way.*

When I was still a preschooler, I unlatched the yard gate, took my younger brother's hand and set out to play mailman. We pretended to gather the letters from the whicker basket that hung near each front door of the eight houses on our block and then returned home. That evening, my brother and I sat on the sun-porch couch, snuggled close to Mother while she read from a McGuffey Reader. *The story was about a fluffy yellow duckling. At the end of the story, the young duckling had learned the importance of listening and obeying her mother's rules for safety. After Mother closed the book she said, "The mother duck in the story had rules to keep her baby safe. Just like the mother duck, your father and I have rules for your safety." Her arms hugged us close. "I'm scared when I look out*

*the window and don't see you both playing in the safety of our
fenced backyard."*

*That night, I dreamed of being that yellow duckling's play-
mate and of being hugged by the warm, soft feathered wings
of mother duck. Years later as a parent, I found myself revising*
The McGuffey *lessons for my own young daughters.*

Preschoolers enjoy imitating other children and adults. They
love to help with simple household tasks, including feeding the
family pet. As with children, routines are important for an animal's well being. Very young children have little control over their
impulse to strike out when they are angry or upset. Therefore, it's
very important for parents to demonstrate how and when to touch
an animal. This groundwork provides a foundation for safe interaction between children and animals. Even with this information,
children under the age of six should still be closely monitored while
they are interacting with the family pet. If a child is too rough
while playing with a pet, parents can call a "time out," explaining
to the child, "What you are doing hurts Dusty, and it makes him
feel very sad. We should never treat him in a way that makes him
feel bad. We need to remember to be gentle with Dusty. For now,
you and Dusty need time apart."

During these early years, children are strongly attached to
transitional objects , a stuffed animal or a special blanket they
can cuddle. These objects are often animated in the child's mind.
Besides being a play buddy, they can serve as a bridge between the
child and the outside world. As the child grows, so does the value
and the depth of different relationships. The friendship with a pet
is a step toward a more mature type of attachment. In addition to
the cuddly stuffed animal, the pet is now a secure and safe haven,
an anchor, for the child to venture into the world. You might say
pets are a living security blanket.

Early Elementary

Elementary school marks the beginning of a child's independence and another step in his or her intellectual development. Children are proud when they succeed in learning new skills at school and are excited to share these accomplishments with Mom and Dad. Each success a child experiences builds his or her self-confidence. School also presents the challenges of a new environment, of a different schedule, and of new activities. Some children take longer than others to adjust to their new surroundings. At the beginning of the school year, some children find a classroom filled with children their own age to be a social and emotional strain. During this confusing time, a companion pet can ease children's frustrations and fears about the world around them.

-Erin McCune

Most elementary schools acknowledge the importance of having a pet center in the classroom. When under stress, a few minutes stroking the soft fur of a rabbit or watching a fish explore the depths of a sea castle can rebalance a child. A problem on the playground

> "Children's self-esteem scores increased significantly over a nine-month period of keeping pets in their school classroom."
>
> -Bergensen

can be forgotten when a teacher invites the child to participate in the care of the schoolroom pet. "Mary, I need your help with the gerbils. I think fresh bedding will make them feel better." Activities like this one are doubly helpful. Caring for the animal helps children feel better about themselves. In addition, when a child becomes involved in a physical activity, the emotional portion of the brain is no longer engaged.

S.L.C. Utah Canine Library Reading Programs

Sandi Martin is a nurse and therapy dog handler. During her therapy rounds at the hospital, she observed how children relaxed during their visits with her therapy dogs. After the visit, the children were happier and more positive about their condition and about life in general. This insight prompted Sandi to consider the role that therapy dogs might play in helping children with reading difficulties.

With the help of her Portuguese water dog, Olivia, Sandi started the Reading Education Assistance Dogs programs in 1997. These dogs do much more than just lend a sympathetic ear. Children with reading difficulties often experience anxieties associated with the struggle of comprehending all of the squiggles on a page. In short, reading is highly stressful for them. As a result, some of the children experience shortness of breath, heart palpitations, and sweaty palms. These symptoms affect the brain's ability to concentrate, further confounding the learning process.

As we discussed earlier, animals, specifically dogs and cats, have a profound effect on human physiology as well as psychology. They slow the heart rate and lower blood pressure. Their mere presence can have a strong influence on counteracting anxiety. When children relax physically, their minds relax as well. This opens their capability to learn and to understand reading.

The dogs used in reading assistance programs have been specially trained. Some dogs will rest a paw on the page encouraging the child to read the whole page. When the trainer says, "Turn," the dog lifts its paw. Some of the dogs stare intently at the page. During their training, various treats were hidden in the pages of the book. The dogs give the children the impression they are hanging on their every word, prompting them to try harder and to read longer and with greater enthusiasm. Sandi says, "It's fun and gets kids to the point that they're so proud of their reading accomplishments that they want to do it again."

The program was so successful that it is now offered in hospital pediatric wards, rehabilitation centers, Headstart, Boys and Girls Clubs, and preschools throughout the country. These "canine reading specialists" not only boost a child's self-esteem; they can also raise their reading level at least one full grade level. In many instances, canine tutors have been found to be more successful in helping children improve their reading skills than their human counterparts. As one elementary student said, "Dogs can't laugh at you when you make mistakes."

At home, animals can encourage reading as well. Parents could suggest beginning students read to their pet. This novel involvement will create the excitement of a new game, one that offers valuable skills for a lifetime. When parents model enthusiasm for reading, children will latch on as well. A child's reading comprehension can be aided when parents ask questions such as "Do you think Fluffy understands what you just read? Tell her what it means."

Pets can also be handy homework helpers. A pet's presence during after-school studies can encourage the student to "stick with it" longer. The animal can also reduce the anxiety associated with the confusion of difficult concepts.

In Webster's Dictionary, the definition of a hero is: "someone who is admired for his or her achievements and qualities."

I think a hero encourages me to want to be a better person and gives hope for a better tomorrow. Heroes come in all shapes and sizes. My hero is small in stature but big in heart. Without saying a word, he brings joy, comfort, and smiles. My hero is a three-foot Shetland pony named Tater Tot, and the joy he brings to the community's grandparents is amazing!

Lemhi County's primary industry has been agriculture. Many of the residents grew up with animals. Some of their best memories include horses and horseback riding. So during Tater Tot's visits, our community's elders get the wonderful gift of reliving some of their best memories. Their hands have forgotten how to do many everyday things, but they quickly remember how to pet a pony.

I recently spent the whole afternoon with my hero. We visited the residents of the Discovery Care Center in Salmon, Idaho. My hero visits weekly with his friends here. I watched as eyes lit up and smiles spread across the faces as each person was reacquainted with my hero.

Tater Tot not only visits the Discovery Care Center, but he also takes part in an after-school program. He participates in a therapeutic riding program, designed for people with physical and mental disabilities.

Tater Tot does not act alone in these activities. He has a group of other community heroes who help transport him to where he needs to go and provide him with everyday care.

Tater Tot is an example of an everyday hero. Tater Tot brings our community closer and teaches us that we don't need words to communicate with each other. He shows, nonverbally, gentle kindness and love for people.

-Bailey Moulton

Handling Frustration

Pets don't always do what a child wants. Although this creates frustration for the child, it opens an opportunity for parents to teach tolerance, respect, and patience. Parents can model respect by showing proper ways to interact with a pet.

One afternoon, Katie was having a tea party with her cat, Mitten. Katie had set all of her stuffed animals in chairs surrounding a small table, and she had one place set for Mitten. Mitten, however, did not want to sit in the small plastic chair. Each time the cat attempted to leave, Katie would wrap her small arms around the cat's middle and plop her back onto the chair. On the third time, Katie frowned and told her cat, "Mitten, sit still for our tea party!" Katie squeezed the cat and tried to hold her in place. Mitten laid back her ears, twitched her tail, and swiped the child's hand. Tears welled in Katie's eyes. Rubbing two red scratches, she cried out, "Bad kitty!"

As parents, our first impulse in a situation like this one is to yell at the cat (or the child). Instead a parent should be focused on preventing a future incident by explaining to the child why the cat reacted as he or she did and do so in a way the child can understand.

"Can you tell me what happened?"

"I want to have a tea party, and kitty won't stay in his chair."

"Some kitties don't like to sit in chairs. Even if they do, they don't like to stay there for long. You get tired of staying in one place don't you?"

The child nods "yes."

"Well, so does kitty. When you try to force kitty to stay in a place he doesn't want to be, you are making kitty angry. When you try and hold onto his tail, it hurts him. When someone pulls your hair, it hurts doesn't it.? Kitty will tell you when he is getting mad. He will lay his ears back flat against his head so tight it will look as if he doesn't have any ears. Kitty's tail will begin to swish back and forth in a very fast manner. These are kitty's ways of telling you that he is mad and that you must stop what you are doing. If you don't, the only way that kitty can get you to stop is to bite or scratch you. Can you remember how kitty tells you that he is getting mad?"

The parent should work with the child until the child can repeat the indicators.

"When kitty is happy, he purrs. We can help him to feel happy by petting him softly and gently like this. You try it. Good job. Now, if we put something nice and soft on the chair and then pet kitty, he might be happy enough to stay in the chair. Remember that kitty may not want to stay in the chair. It's important to let kitty go if he is not happy. You wouldn't make your best friend, Jenny, stay if she was crying and unhappy would you?"

"No, I'd let her go home"

"Right, you are a good friend. Good friends help their friends to feel happy. Kitty is your friend, too."

Adolescence

As young people enter adolescence, they begin to understand their uniqueness. They start to explore special interests, develop close friendships, and become more involved in social activities. Because they have a strong need to feel accepted, they will often dress and talk like their peers. Through this process, they learn about their personal strengths and weaknesses. Play is important. They engage in various activities such as sports and video games. Since their attention span increases at this age, the child may work hard to perfect a skill. Training the family pet can be an enjoyable and exciting new skill for an adolescent to learn. Clubs such as 4-H can be a way to blend social time with the training and helps to make the activity even more fun. Sometimes as the adolescent becomes more involved in training, he or she loses perspective and therefore make training a chore or a very serious competition. When it is approached in this fashion, it not only loses its enjoyment but also can often drive a wedge in the relationship between the youngster and the pet. This can be avoided by keeping the training approach playful, a game. Both children and animals enjoy games.

Although social groups are very important to the young person, misunderstandings can develop due to the different maturity levels. Quarreling with friends or being left out of a social function is common. Young people wonder why classmates are their friends one day and the next day they ignore them. It is often difficult for adolescents to understand the fickleness of teenage social interactions.

The concept of fairness is a large part of adolescent thinking. Relating back to nature can help the child to understand many aspects of life, but fairness is not always one of them. It may not seem fair for a baby antelope to die under the claw of a lioness, but that is often how the event plays out. It is important for children to understand that they have no control over how someone will act. It is not their fault that a friend now ignores them during recess.

They do not have control over anyone's thoughts or feelings other than their own. Things will happen in life that they may consider unfair, that cannot be changed. The one thing children do have control over is how they choose to react to the situation. They can choose to let it permanently upset them or to let it go. This is a valuable lesson that, once learned, will serve them for the rest of their lives. It is not an easy one. It takes lots of practice and requires many repetitions of the explanation "You do not have control over what happens in life, but you can choose how you will respond to what happens."

Many preteens begin the bodily changes associated with puberty. These rapid physical changes may sap their energy. This is often why parents complain about the apparent laziness of their child. It is not uncommon for this child to experience awkward body movements due to this fast growth. Sometimes they experience physical discomfort such as aching limbs, headaches, or odd appetite requests. Preteens' interest in their changing body may be expressed with questions such as "How do bones grow? What makes my hair brown? How come I have freckles?"

> *Nurturing animals is particularly beneficial for boys. This may be due to the fact traditional families encourage nurturing behavior from girls, caring for babies, babysitting, caring for the home. Boys are expected to act manly. The care of animals is an acceptable way for boys to display and explore their softer nature.*
>
> -Vlasta Vizek
> Vidovic (1999)

As preteens become more in touch with their emotions, they may feel alienated thinking that no one understands what they are experiencing. They are relieved to find out others experience frustration, fear, anger, and shyness. During this time of rapid emotional change, it is important for parents to exemplify open and nonjudgmental communication. Unfortunately this is not easy. Young people often cannot express what they are feeling either because they cannot put it into words or because they are embarrassed to do so. Involving the family pet can help unlock the block and help them to express their feelings and their concerns. Interacting with the animal will often act as a conduit through which children feel they can safely talk to their parents. This can be done in a couple of ways. If parents sense that the child needs some time alone to formulate his or her thoughts, they can suggest that the child take the family dog for a walk or perhaps ride the horse. If parents sense that the child is ready to talk but perhaps doesn't quite know how to begin, they can suggest the child join them in grooming a pet or in cleaning the animal's enclosure. These simple and repetitive tasks are therapeutic for both the parent and the child. The animal and not the child becomes the center of attention. When the pressure is removed, the child feels safer to express his or her emotions.

Something was bothering Ethan. When I asked what was wrong he told me, "Nothing," and then went to his room and shut the door. I looked at Ginger lying on the living room rug. Sensing my eyes on her, she thumped her tail in a steady beat. "OK girl, time to work your magic." I patted my leg and the sweet golden retriever came to my side. Together we walked down the hall to Ethan's room. I opened the door and motioned for Ginger to enter, then closed the door behind her. I gave them about ten minutes together, knowing that Ginger would demand attention and affection from Ethan, drawing his emotions to the surface.

Then, I went to the cupboard and took out Ginger's brushes. Knocking softly on Ethan's door, I entered the room. Ethan sat on the floor, cradling Ginger on his lap. The golden rolled her eyes in my direction, but other than that, didn't move. I sat next to Ethan and without a word, I handed him one of the brushes. In silence we worked on Ginger's coat, smoothing the fur and teasing out knots. We finished brushing one side when Ethan spoke. "I didn't get it." He didn't look up from Ginger.

I kept working. "The part in the play?"

"Yeah. I really didn't want it anyway."

"I'm sorry honey. I know how hard you worked on your audition. You put in a lot of time to make sure you were well prepared."

"They told me I was great; the director seemed really pleased with my audition. I just don't get it. What happened?" Ethan had stopped brushing and was searching my face for an answer, one that I didn't have to give. I followed his lead and laid my brush aside, scooted closer to him and folded my arms around his shoulders. I felt his tears dampen my shirt. He had tried so hard not to cry, to be the man he was growing into and not to succumb to the boy he still was. I held him until the boy faded and the man took hold again. Sensing this shift, I reluctantly eased my hold, giving him the option of staying or moving away. Ethan whipped the tears from his eyes. Ginger tucked her nose under Ethan's free hand and moved it until it rested on her head.

"Ethan, I'm not sure why the director changed her mind and selected someone else for the part. But I know that you did your best; you did your part. If you want, we could call the director and ask her how you could improve the next time. Perhaps she can give you some tips that will improve your chances for next time. You could also let her know that if someone drops out or if she needs an extra, you are still interested in participating. How does that sound?"

"Okay, I guess. Do you think I might get a part?"

"I really don't know, but if we don't make the call and try, you definitely won't, and we won't learn anything to improve on."

Ethan absently stroked Ginger's head. "You're right. I'll go and get her phone number from my backpack."

For children to trust in themselves and to acquire self-confidence, they must feel secure as they develop emotionally. Confiding in a pet can help a child feel less frustrated during this confusing time. Confidence and self-esteem allow the child to separate emotionally from parents and become independent.

Adolescence is the time when parents fall from superhero status. Children begin to see their parents as people with flaws and, therefore, may be over critical. As harsh as it is for parents to hear phrases of independence, it is all part of the process. This is a continuation of the child becoming autonomous. While they may want or expect help from their parents, they are growing in independence and resent being told what to do.

The routine of caring for an animal can provide a balance during these unstable times. Pets provide a feeling of purpose and a sense of security. They offer nonjudgmental listening and unconditional love. The child's interest in a pet may expand beyond furry friendship and develop into a working partnership or hobby. Youth groups such as 4-H or different breed clubs can help children learn how to give and to receive criticism and compliments. They provide camaraderie and promote both teamwork and healthy competition. They are a good environment for children to learn how to handle success and failure gracefully.

Early high school years are self-centered years. "Who am I?" becomes the big question. The adolescent is sandwiched between the conflicting pressures of conforming to peer culture and meeting adult expectations. This can create stress and emotional turmoil. Some youth gracefully handle this pressure while others are unnerved by it.

In addition, adolescence is a time of wild emotional changes, and the fluxes can be dramatic. Boys and girls become more interested in each other. Crushes, intense friendships, and hero worship are common as boys and girls spend more time together. Their moods may fluctuate, the adolescent feeling confident one day and insecure the next. They often alternate between being generous and mature to being selfish and immature. When an adolescent talks about the fear, anxieties, and perplexities in his or her life, parents need to be good listeners rather than advice givers. Although this is true for any time a parent interacts with a child, it is especially important during this time because young teens desperately need to feel as though they are living their own life and that they are fully supported by their parents in their decision to do so. At this time, school may take a second seat to social activities. As a result, some students may fall behind academically. Although parents will want and should encourage academic achievement, they must real-

ize that this is a phase that most all young teens go through.

Maturity levels vary drastically during this developmental phase. Girls tend to mature more quickly than boys; however, there are maturation differences even within the two genders. Because of this, sports can be awkward, especially for boys. During this time, the child is turning into an adult and adolescents often find the changes occurring in their body disturbing. Both boys and girls can experience frustration if their bodies develop more slowly than their friends.

As with the younger years, the nurturing qualities of an animal companion can assist the teen in handling confused feelings during the period of intense change. A pet provides the unconditional ear and nonjudgmental love that is so needed during these tumultuous times. Interacting with the family pet is often the perfect salve for a bruised or confused spirit.

Young Adult

By high school, the young person is fully in the grip of adolescence. This is a period of personal quest. Where do I fit in the world? What do I do with my life? The pre-adult is trying to tailor his or her identity.

This is also a time when childhood games and books are tucked away. The family pet can be a touchstone from childhood. Even through the veneer of adulthood, teens harbor their tender child. It is this part that still needs protection from the drastically changing world around them. A pet provides relief from the pressure to live up to adult expectations and accepts the teen unconditionally.

Teens empathize with their pets as well as feel that the animal understands their deepest feelings. In times of turmoil, they may lean on this special connection. "Pets perform heroic rescues daily by being present in times of human need."(Dr. Marty Becker)

A dear friend of mine came from an abusive childhood in which both parents were alcoholics. She is certain that her childhood dog was, in fact, an angel. The collie was her steadfast companion from the time that she came into her life, a rejected show dog, until my friend graduated from high school. Among the many things this collie taught her, the memory that rings the clearest is the lesson of unconditional love. My friend admits she was often deeply hurt by the world around her, and although she loved her dog, she would vent her feelings on the only one who steadfastly loved her. The dog never sulked or cowered away from the anger of the confused child. My friend knows that she felt her hurt and loved her all the more for it.

The day after my friend graduated from high school and left the abusive environment forever, her childhood angel returned to heaven, her work on earth completed.

- Christine Hamer

Teenage years are often confusing and worrisome for parents as well. They are filled with anxieties too. Parents may find themselves regretting things said in the heat of an argument. Self-doubt may arise. Are they doing "it" right? Just like all other phases of child rearing, there is no one right way to go through the process. Although all teenagers face a variety of developmental issues, how they deal with them depends on their unique personality and life experiences. As teenagers strive for independence, parents may note many of the following feelings and behaviors.

Teenagers worry about being normal. They often fluctuate between poor self-concept and high personal expectations. As a result, they experience mood swings. Shyness and modesty may appear. Their friends tend to define the teens' taste in clothing and music and can strongly influence their behavior. Their interest in the opposite sex increases beyond what they felt as preteens. They change relationships frequently but also develop long lasting friendships. They identify with their parents' faults and realize they, too, have imperfections. Unlike when they were preteens, young adults will tell their parents if they feel as though the parent is interfering with their new-found independence. Because they are balancing between childhood and adulthood, when under stress, they may revert to the familiarity of childish behavior. Parents may note that their young adult has an increased ability to work both mentally and physically. As a result, it is common for parents to see an improvement in the teen academically.

Parenting is difficult. We are constantly faced with choices of how and when to respond to our children's behaviors. "Do I intervene in this problem, or should I let the child work it out?" Jeffrey S. Katz, PhD, a clinical psychologist, says, "If a parent tends to rescue youngsters when a problem arises, the child does not experience the consequences of his own behavior. They do not learn from what they do but learn that they can always blame something or someone else for what happens to them." Although parents need to be there to provide direction, taking a "hands-off" approach will encourage the child to problem solve and make their own decisions. Parents can show children how to look at problems. They can explore different solutions with their teen and the merits and pitfalls of the various choices. We can help them to acquire realistic expectations for outcomes. This will provide an opportunity for them to learn about their own weaknesses and strengths and to develop positive coping skills. This being said, it is important not to thwart a teen's desire to tackle an overly ambitious project.

> *My boys are avid student filmmakers. During the process of planning their projects, some of their visions seemed, both to me and to my husband, based in teen fantasy rather than reality. Although we were tempted to throw a "wet blanket" on some of their ideas, we learned very quickly that not only would our nay-saying become grounds for a battle, but also we were often amazed at what the boys were able to accomplish when left to their own devices. In their most recent film, the script (written by my eldest) called for a helicopter. When I questioned him about the logistics surrounding obtaining one, he told me that not only did he require a helicopter; he needed a Vietnam era chopper. The only thing that my husband and I said was that finding one might prove to be a bit of a challenge. We allowed the boys to do all of their own searching, phone calling, e-mailing. We offered suggestions and support but let them do all of the work and discovery. After seven months of searching, they obtained the chopper they needed for the scene. The seemingly impossible became reality.*

On the other hand, if the parent observes a conflict escalating where serious harm could result, he or she should stop the confrontation and give assistance to resolve the dispute. Sometimes children will take out their frustration and/or anger by hitting/ kicking a family member or their pet. As parents, we need to let them know this is not acceptable behavior. For example, we might say something such as "I know you're upset at your brother for breaking your model airplane, but kicking him is not the way to solve your problem. You need to let Dad or me know what's happening. We can help you choose another way to handle the situation so no one gets hurt. Your brother can buy you another plane from his allowance. However, you'll have an extra chore tonight for choosing to punish your brother instead of coming to us."

As a parent, it's important to take time to assess how your feelings may affect your reaction to your child. In the heat of the moment, thoughtless words can strike a harsh criticism. Using words such as "You dummy!" or "You can't do anything right," are damaging phrases that will injury a child's self image. Before you speak, take a deep breath and remember that your child's behavior is not directed to you. It is important to focus on the situation, not the child. "When you scream at me, it hurts my ears, and I can't understand what you need. If you can talk softly, then I can help you."

As parents, we are builders. Construction is noisy, dirty work. Sometimes with all of the parts scattered around the worksite, it looks as though the child will never be a finished structure. Then almost miraculously, the process seems to take on a life of its own. But as with a building, the strength of the adult we are helping to build will be dependent on the tools and materials that we use. We are helping our children construct lifelong qualities such as personal freedom and inner peace. These tools can help to restore emotional balance to our young adults during times of turmoil. What tools and raw materials will you offer your children as you work to craft the next generation?

When we embrace a love for animals, we expand our love and caring for all living beings. The more each person expands, the greater the chance for our world to survive. In ancient times, certain animals were revered for magical virtues and powers that helped mankind. This mystical need for animals remains deep in the human soul. Personal testimonies now supported by scientific studies prove that our connection to companion animals offers a profound healing effect on the human body, mind, and spirit.

Responsibility

Most parents believe that having one or more family pets provides a positive experience for their children. In fact, homes with at least one child account for more than ninety percent of all pet ownership. It is generally reasoned that raising a pet will be a good life lesson and it will teach responsibility. There is growing evidence that a child's involvement with a pet does, in fact, have a multi-facetted impact on the child's growth and development.

Caring for a pet helps establish certain habits such as tidiness, punctuality, and self-discipline. These are valuable skills needed both at home and in school. Robert Poresky, Associate Professor of Family Studies and Human Services at Kansas State University, recounts, "In one study, we found that three- and four-year-olds with pets were better able to understand the feelings of other children than those without pets."

As we said earlier, the responsibility of pet ownership begins before you acquire your new family companion. Researching different pets and discussing the acquisition as a family before you buy will send a positive message to your children. It shows them that you are serious about the responsibility of adding an additional life to the family and that it isn't a decision that you take lightly.

Children often have fantasies about having an animal friend. However these dreams don't include the mundane chores associated with pet care. Their thoughts are more on the lines of the play and fun they will have with their new pet. Dr Zimmerman, a psychologist in Florida, cautions that choosing to "own" and take care of another life is a heavy responsibility. If done correctly, it can be one of the most important life lessons of a child's experience.

My friends Bianca and Paige and I were playing at Bianca's house, and we got into a huge fight. So when I came home crying, my dog Albi came in the room and he sat, and he licked my face.

My friends and I didn't play together for a long time. So Albi and I did a lot together. We would pass the Ball, eat together and even slept together!

My friends and I made up in a month, but for that month Albi and I were best friends!

We had to put him to sleep in March 2000. Now when my friends and me get in a fight I think of him!

-Lauren Whisonant
Grade 5

To help your child align his or her dreams with reality, talk with your child before you get your pet. One way to help children understand the responsibility they are about to undertake is by using an old health class strategy. A hard-boiled egg or stuffed animal can be a teaching substitute for a live pet. Establish care-giving rules that would be similar to the pet you are considering adopting, such as regular potty breaks for a puppy or regular cage cleaning and handling time for small animals. "Puddles" from unattended pretend pets could be staged for older children to clean up. Although there is positive interactions between a real live pet and your child, if you find that you are battling for the care of the "stand-in," consider whether the family is prepared to make the commitment a real pet would require.

Dr. Louise Davis, a child and family development specialist with Mississippi State University Extension Service, says the best way to teach children responsibility is through mirroring that behavior ourselves. "Children watch everything we do. Parents should show their children that the pet has to be cared for everyday." The success of a child-animal bond lies largely on the willingness of adults to act as parents to both child and pet. Raising outstanding children and great pets requires time and commitment.

The New Pet

When your pet first comes home, everyone is excited. There are more helping hands offered than jobs to be done. But once the novelty of pet ownership wears off, the children often vanish. Older siblings are busy with other obligations, and the younger children whine about being dragged away from the television or X-Box. Chores that were fun when the pet first arrived home are now considered work. At this point, even the simple task of feeding Fido can turn into a battle of paramount proportions.

It is generally the mother who assumes the role of caregiver not only for the children but for the household pets as well. As mothers ourselves, we know the fine art of multi-tasking. We also know most mothers are forced to wear many different hats in a day. Often we find ourselves physically and emotionally drained, unable to tackle even one more battle. An unhappy child is more irritating than a mosquito. Frustrated parents wanting to get the job done succumb to the young whiners. The lesson that we wanted to teach our children, such as the all-important one of commitment, can be buried like Fido's unwanted bones after the first steady week of arguments. If, as in most American families, the parents are time-stressed, the additional chore of caring for a pet may be more than they are willing to handle, and the poor pet may find himself up for adoption. Taking over your child's work may seem to be the easiest solution. After all, adults can get the work done more efficiently, thereby shortening the time commitment to the project. But remember, we are not just caring for our animals; we are also nurturing our children. Although it is much easier to avoid all of the groans, moans, whines, and woes, doing the work for our children robs them of a chance to learn. Life is interdependent. The honor of caring for another is one of the greatest gifts we can give. It is an integral part of life.

Harmony can be restored to a frustrated household if parents implement basic guidelines to be followed by all family members.

Establish a chore chart. (See Appendix 1.) List every task needed for your pet's well-being, from cleaning the cage to giving the daily allotment of hugs and kisses. Assign each person in the family a job or perhaps a block of jobs. Although parents need to help younger family members, allow the child to do the chore.

Parents should rely on a chore chart until a routine is established. Once a task is completed, the "chore doer" can mark off the appropriate square. To add fun and color, charts can be marked with stars or stickers or colored with crayons. Jobs can be rotated weekly so less desirable chores, such as cleaning cages, are shared by all.

Demonstrate and guide verbally. Explain each chore thoroughly so that your child understands the details involved in each task. "The parakeet's cage needs cleaning. You can spread the newspaper. We'll work together." When the job is finished, you might say, "Look what we did together! I really appreciate your help." Because children understand better by imitating and by doing than they do by listening, do each step together as you talk. This will also give the child a visual of what a good and completed job looks like.

Depending on the age of the child, parents may need to show how to do a task correctly many times. Parents can quiz their child as they do the chore together by saying such things as, "Tell me what I should do next." Before the child attempts any task alone, the parent and child should switch roles, with the child doing the chore and explaining to the parent how the job should be done.

First praise what the child did right. If corrections need to be made in a child's work, first praise what the child did right, then almost as an afterthought, the parent can add that it might be better next time if the child did…this or that. "Mary, I really like the way that you saw the kitty's litter box needed cleaning. I was proud that you remembered how important it is for us to keep the box clean. Remember how we talked about how sensitive kitty is to smells, especially in her litter box? That's why we need to clean all of the waste from the box. Sometimes that means we dump the entire box, clean it, and put in fresh litter. Next time before you clean the box, why don't we look at it together and decide what should be done?" It is important for parents to differentiate important care issues from personal preference. For instance, it doesn't matter if a child feeds the animal first or changes the water first as long as both are done.

Resist the urge to jump in. Sometimes a child will struggle to accomplish a task. Resist the urge to jump in and do the chore yourself. Let's not lose sight of the primary objective. We are developing relationships not only between our child and pet but also between our child and ourselves. Work beside your child and give encouragement, but it is important the child completes his or her chore. Every child needs the feeling of self-satisfaction, the sense of "I can do it" that comes from success.

Keep tasks age appropriate.

Toddlers and preschoolers. For young children, helping an animal can give a sense of satisfaction and self-fulfillment. Jobs need to be age appropriate and parents should give specific directions, for example, "Mary, please put the dog food in Buffy's dish." From about two to five years of age, and with adult supervision, children can help fill water dishes and food bowls for cats and dogs. They can feed fish or give fresh water and food to a hamster, a gerbil, or a mouse. With a little adult supervision, children can have loads of fun by pulling a string for a kitten to chase or throwing a ball for a dog during playtime.

If you have a dog, feeding time can be a good time to help the young child do some simple training. Even young children can teach a dog how to sit and wait before getting its meal. Although you may have to hold the food dish so the dog doesn't knock it out of your child's hands, your child can say "sit." Exemplify patience with the dog and the child. When the dog responds, let the youngster place the dish down for the dog. This simple training session teaches the dog that he also needs to take directions from even the youngest family member. It gently and effectively places the pet in the proper position in the family hierarchy. According to Wayne Hunthausen, DVM, "A young pup needs to learn two things about children right away: Children have control over it, and the children are the good guys."

School Age. Children ages six to eight can help with additional chores. At this age, a child is just beginning to understand that a pet has his or her own unique language. Take advantage of your child's natural curiosity and observation skills. A little time spent watching and talking about your pet with your child will enhance your relationship with both. Children with in the ages eight to twelve understand that animals can feel pain and fear. As your child grows, the number of chores should also increase. Children generally enjoy that they can provide for and comfort their pet. By participating in these activities, they can feel pride in their work. They might enjoy holding the leash while you take the dog for walks and can participate in adult supervised obedience training lessons.

Successfully training a pet will help a child to gain self-confidence. It also teaches patience, self-control, and delayed gratification. (See the chapter "Pets Teach Tolerance" for more about training your pet.)

More mature older members of this age group can assume total care of easy starter pets although the thoroughness of the tasks should still be monitored. For the animal's welfare, it is important that parents check to insure optimal care. However, it is equally important that your children not feel as though you are constantly "looking over their shoulder. " Rather than chastise your child for an incomplete or poor job, explain how the lack of care affects the animal. Children love and relate to stories, especially ones that involve animals. Telling a story about two animals, one that had good care and one that had poor care, can instruct your child without a personal attack to self-esteem. Involving their empathy and emotions will ensure that they remember the lesson much longer than if they are merely told what they did wrong. One of the values of pet ownership is the development of an intrinsic motivation to care for another because of feelings of love and empathy.

Parents can use companion animals as a tool for teaching children to think about the consequences of

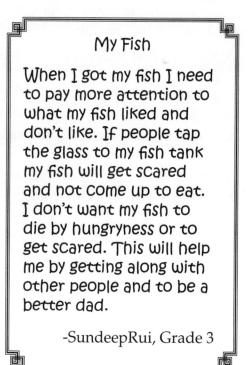

My Fish

When I got my fish I need to pay more attention to what my fish liked and don't like. If people tap the glass to my fish tank my fish will get scared and not come up to eat. I don't want my fish to die by hungryness or to get scared. This will help me by getting along with other people and to be a better dad.

-SundeepRui, Grade 3

their actions and make constructive choices. Sometimes a parent won't need to say anything. A pet's reaction to a child's inappropriate behavior (assuming that the situation poses no threat for either the animal or the child) may get the point across all on its own. After the fact, a parent may help the child sort out the cause of the animal's reaction.

Interactions with animals can positively influence the moral development of a child.   A child's compassion toward animals is directly related to his or her empathy toward people. Further, children's awareness of how their behavior impacts a family pet will also directly influence their interrelationships with other children. For example, when children assume responsibility for a pet's care, they learn compassion as they respond to their pet's needs. In turn, this translates to understanding the feelings and needs of people. This awareness will also enhance other forms of pro-social behaviors.

According to Poresky, just having a pet in the home isn't good enough for the child to derive these benefits. The child must become involved with the pet in order for the relationship to have a positive impact on the child's development.

Teenage Children. Older children can assist younger ones as coaches and mentors as well as personally accepting responsibility for a task on the chore chart. Teenagers often have interests outside the home. However, the family pet still needs care. This is a good time for parents to reinforce that responsibility for a pet continues throughout the life of the animal, not just at the convenience of the teen.

Parents commonly equate children learning responsibility with the regular feeding and care of the family pet. Although reliability is important, it is not the only lesson to be learned. We are helping our children uphold the commitments they make to us, to their pet, and most important, to themselves. By keeping a promise to do a chore or care for a pet, children make deposits in their personal integrity bank. The wealth of this account directly corresponds to the children's self-esteem and belief in themselves. Each time a child makes a commitment and then keeps it, even if from a parent's insistence, he or she grows this self-esteem account and learns about personal integrity, commitment, and responsibility.

One day, a very bright teen sat down with his calculator and began to add the different products needed to create his family's bountiful garden: the cost of the plants, the cost of the fertilizer, tools, water, cages, and vine poles. He added a small stipend for the work provided by himself and that of his siblings.

He checked his figures twice. Surely he had made an error. There were a lot of children in his family, therefore, he reasoned, the cost of food must be the reason that he and his siblings were required to toil every summer in the family garden. But according to his calculations, the family was losing money! Even factoring out the labor of the children, it would still be much cheaper to purchase the vegetables at the local market. This young man played visions of being the hero among the family. His brothers and sisters would hold a party to celebrate their liberation from the seasonal chore.

Armed with numbers, he presented his case.

His father listened quietly to the entire explanation and dutifully studied the figures presented as evidence. When the young man had finished, his father put his arm around his shoulders and smiled at his industrious son.

"You've done a lot of work here son. I'm very impressed with your ability to calculate the cost of our produce and you're absolutely right. It would be much less expensive for us to purchase our produce through the store. But you see son, I'm not just raising vegetables in this garden. I'm raising young men and women.

Yes, it is hard to be a parental oak in the face of an emotional storm, but it's okay to make children do things they don't want to, including chores. The more times you stand behind a household rule, the more established it becomes. Then, just like taking a shower or brushing our teeth, the guidelines for feeding, walking, brushing, and playing with the family pet can become healthy habits.

I have two boys, twelve and fifteen. They are responsible for a variety of farm chores, including caring for two horses, ten laying hens, three dogs, a cat, and a parakeet. Mucking through barnyard mud on rainy Washington days isn't fun, and I regularly hear arguments rumble between the two boys about whose turn it is to feed and care for the critters. However, even if one of my boys leaves the house in a foul mood, he returns rejuvenated in spirit. It is virtually impossible to remain upset or angry while stroking the soft warmth of an animal. Caring for a being who responds with bountiful joy to the simple pleasures of an armful of hay, clean water, and a bowlful of fresh food enhances everyone's life. The nonjudgmental love given by animals is a gift that every child should experience.

- Christine Hamer

Some schools have recognized the multi-faceted advantage of involving children with animals. A high school in Indianapolis is pairing "at risk" teens with shelter dogs that need some obedience training before they can be successfully placed into homes. This non-traditional, program entitled "Paws and Think," has helped the adolescents develop patience, self-confidence, and responsibility. These young people are aware that their work is more than an exercise designed for school. Their success or failure may dictate the fate of a dog. This raises responsibility to a whole new level. Not only are they responsible for the care and training of their canine companion; they also are responsible for its life. As one student in an article by Kim Hooper stated, "It makes us work harder to get them trained, so they won't be put to sleep."

I grew up on a small ranch in Montana. Before my sisters or I were allowed to eat dinner, it was our responsibility to care for the various farm animals. My parents explained that domestic animals rely on us to take care of them. They cannot go to the store and buy food, nor can they draw water from the well to fill their bucket. By choosing to have animals, we accept the responsibility for their care and welfare. This philosophy is one I have taken with me into adulthood and passed on to my own children. To this day, our family does not sit down for supper until the animals are fed and bedded down for the night, the value of selflessness taught in a subtle but powerful lesson.

- Christine Hamer

By teaching our children the value of keeping a personal promise we help them to experience the intrinsic rewards that come from caring for dependent lives. Assuming responsibility, at its deepest level means children learn to be responsible for themselves, for their actions and hopefully for the global community. As parents, we must devote the time and energy needed to create compassionate people. It is *our* responsibility to put the "kind" back in mankind, one child at a time.

Spring Garden

It wasn't an invitation for a social gathering
Me pulling weeds in the spring garden
Sitting on pavers
Prying dandelions and clover from the wooly thyme and
Irish moss.
It wasn't an invitation
To throw
Your buried stick
Or the chewed plastic water bottle
Or even the discarded sod pieces I had put in the bucket
With the other weeds.
It wasn't an invitation to sit on my lap
And lick the sweat from my face.
But persistently
You made it just that:
A reminder

                - Molly McNulty

PETS TEACH TOLERANCE

We cannot live through a day without impacting the world around
us, and we have a choice: What sort of impact do we want to make?
And it is not only humans who matter as individuals
—so too do animals.

- Jane Goodall
A Reason for Hope

Some of the best lessons in tolerance come from the mothers of the animal kingdom. A mother dog, for instance, shows tremendous tolerance for the playful antics of her young litter as the pups tumble about, pulling on her ears and tail with their very sharp puppy teeth. However, she doesn't hesitate to discipline them when the play enters the realm of rudeness. She is a fair teacher of the rules of the canine society. Teaching is a test of patience.

In order for us to understand patience and tolerance, we will need to explore more than the interactions between a mother and her brood. In the most basic sense, patience is the ability to suppress emotional expression in a stressful situation. This ability, in the case of mothers, is drawn out by instinct. For instance, a mother dog might inhibit a bite that would harm her offspring. For most people, patience does not come naturally. Rather, it is a skill that is learned and one that is tested daily by our interactions with coworkers, our patience in the check-out lines, and our tolerance for traffic snarls. We can help our children acquire this very important skill by teaching them to control acting out on their counterproductive impulses.

Feelings of frustration and anger are natural, but they are not the fault of or caused by another person or by a pet; instead, they are the reactions of the individual to certain situations and under that person's control. Coaching children about appropriate ways to manifest their feelings is a good first step in their understanding of emotions. The better we equip our children with the resources to identify with their feelings, the better they will handle emotional situations without feeling undue stress.

Taking Care of My Dog

My dog is not so easy to tack care of. My dog poops in the house. Me and my brother have to clean it all up. Our dog also poops out side in our backyard. We have to clean it up to. We also have to feed the dog a lot.

When we first got the dog I really really wanted to do all those chores. Exept when I started to do them. I really wished I didn't say that from now on I have to tack care of my dog and what I learned from that was it is   werth it to tack care of my dog. Because I will almas love my dog!

And I never want her to Die!!!

-Alec Dennis, Grade 3

Let your child know that you also have these feelings. Explain some of the positive ways you have developed to deal with these emotions. Perhaps you are still learning to handle certain aspects of your personality. It's okay to be honest, especially with older children. Let them know that personal improvement doesn't end with adulthood; rather, it is a lifelong process.

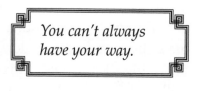

You can't always have your way.

Talking about different emotions and the appropriate release of feelings is very important for children when interacting with animals. For small animals, a hit or aggressive squeeze from a frustrated child can be harmful or even deadly. Dogs and cats may be forced into self-defense, either biting or scratching the child.

It takes time to develop a relationship with an animal. Sometimes it feels like an eternity before we establish even the most basic rapport. I recommend that children keep a notebook of all aspects of their pet's care. The research that the family did before the pet was acquired can be in the beginning of the notebook. If the pet is already a part of the family, perhaps the child can research the natural history of the animal or the origin of the pet's particular breed. The whole family can become involved in learning the biology and behavior of your pet. Keeping a journal of interesting things the animal does can provide a fun read in the future. (More on behavior journaling is in the next section, "Before Training Your Animal.)

Keep records on your animal's behavior. It is imperative for your pet's well-being that you understand how it shows discomfort, joy, and fear, in short, how it communicates. Since your pet can't tell you when it isn't feeling well, a change in its behavior is often your only indicator of illness. Becoming acutely aware of your pet's routines and behaviors is an important gauge when determining its health.

Coach your child to be patient with a shy or fearful response from his new pet. Small pets such as mice, parakeets, hamsters, and gerbils are most often frightened when they arrive in their new home. Moving slowly and sitting quietly are big tests of patience for younger children. The child will be rewarded, as a pet's curiosity draws the animal into exploring its surroundings.

Training a pet is another way for children to acquire important life skills. Good trainers develop a relationship with their animal, becoming a leader rather than a master. To do this will take time, skill, and patience. The goal is to engage the animal's intellect and cooperation rather than force its compliance.

According to Poresky, "A dog or cat won't always do what the child wants [it] to do, and that can be very important [for the child to understand]. This helps kids learn that there are other perspectives and ways of looking at things."

Before Training Your Animal

Before you begin to teach your animal, you must learn how animals communicate. They "talk" with one another using their body language and facial expressions. Every animal has a sophisticated communication system that conveys important messages such as "I'm the one in charge of this space " or "I'm scared" or "Leave me alone. " Sometimes they inadvertently relay information to other animals watching them, for instance when a rabbit tells a fox or coyote, "I'm going to run now. "

To gain an understanding of your pet's language, it's fun to act like a scientist. Try this simple exercise. Pretend that you are anthropologists and are exploring a new territory in some far away land. You have heard that there are strange and wonderful beings there. They don't look or act much like you, but they have a complex system of communication, and you are challenged with trying to crack the code. You are excited to discover this new language. Both you and your child should each take a notebook and pencil and sit in a quiet place to watch your pet. This is easier with animals that are confined to a cage and can present a bit more of a challenge when observing your cat, dog, horse, or other highly mobile animal. Record every detail that you see. Pay special attention to your animal's gait, the way in which it holds or move its ears, eyes, and mouth. Observe distinct body postures. Try to avoid making emotional judgments regarding your pet's mood. Remember you're scientists exploring a new culture; you know nothing about these creatures.

After you have watched your pet for a period, say about fifteen minutes, compare notes. The detail that a child sees is always amazing. Praise and encourage whatever observations your child makes and add your own. There is no right or wrong in this exercise- it is a process of discovery. This assignment is one worth repeating several times until you both feel as though you have a better understanding of your pet and his behavior. The more accurately you can understand your pet's behavior, the better trainer you will be.

In addition to behavioral notes, keep a training journal. This not only helps to map out the training course but also provides a wonderful reminder of how far your child and his or her pet have come together. It is very encouraging to read from the journal on days when training has been difficult and your child may feel as though the pet is not progressing.

Another good exercise can teach your child the beginnings of budgets and money handling skills. This, too, can be a part of the pet journal that you and your child are keeping.

Help your child set up an expense chart and log everything that is spent on your pet. Set up a budget; perhaps a monthly allocation of money. At the end of the month, you and your child can balance the budget. If you have gone over, together you can search for the reason why. Extra toys can be downsized but basic needs cannot. You may have to adjust the monthly allowance if you find that you are not able to cover your pet's basic care. Record-keeping is a beneficial exercise on many levels. It supports organizational skills, encourages attention to details, and requires consistency, all of which are important in everyday adult life.

Before your child begins training his or her pet, sit down together and write out a training plan in your journal. Record exactly what you are intending to accomplish. Be as specific as possible. Think little and build to bigger. It is not fair to either your child or your pet to try to accomplish too much in any one training session. For help in designing a practical training plan, either contact a local trainer of your type of pet or check out some of the references at the end of this book. Help the child trainer to develop a clear visual image in his or her mind of the daily goal. This will help to keep the child on track when the pet does everything but what he or she is trying to teach. It will also help to see progress as the child reaches toward this goal.

After each lesson, sit down with the child and record what worked and what didn't. What could you do the next time to help your pet succeed? Modify your training plan as necessary. Here is where a good professional trainer can be invaluable. Together, the three of you can evaluate the animal's progress and make the necessary adjustments to the training.

Remember that verbal language is a human trait so speak little or not at all when working with an animal. Let the unspoken communication develop between the child and pet. If you have a bird, cat, dog, or a horse, we highly recommend that you find a good trainer to work with. A few lessons with an experienced individual can save hours of frustration.

Patience is required to build a trusting rapport with an animal. It is also necessary for teaching and practicing the skill you are trying to teach the animal. Often many repetitions are required before the animal understands what is being asked of it. When a child is the primary teacher, it is important for him or her to understand that when animals refuse to do something asked of them, they don't do so to anger or frustrate the child. Perhaps the child isn't teaching in a way that the animal can understand. They may be using improper timing of reinforcement so the animal makes the wrong association. The association (cue and expected response from the animal) might be weak and need more reinforcement. These are all indicators that more time needs to be spent on training. They are not displays of belligerence. Most important, it is just a step in a process and is certainly not a signal of failure for either the trainer or the animal.

Each training exercise should be repeated many times to be sure that the animal fully understands what the child is teaching. Add new concepts in small simple steps. Most errors in training are breaches in communication. These happen when we assume the animal (or child) understands what is expected.

Children easily become frustrated with themselves and their pets. It can be discouraging when a young trainer has devoted time and energy working with an animal and feels as though the animal just isn't getting the idea. It may seem to the child as though an animal is purposefully making him or her look and feel foolish. This can be very exasperating. Many times children are more upset with themselves and their inability to accomplish their goal immediately than they are with the animal. Tolerance and patience with ourselves is a powerful lesson.

As parents, we must help the young trainer keep any temporary setback in the training process in the proper perspective. Some children are willing to laugh at the animal's antics, keeping a sense of humor about themselves and the situation. Others find the process very frustrating and are more likely to succumb to the flow of emotions. Children need to be taught a proper way to vent their feelings. Parents should  monitor training sessions to be sure that anger is never directed toward the pet. The ability to recognize frustration, anger, and ego and to correctly handle these feelings rather than acting out on them is a giant step toward maturity.

Help both child and pet to complete training sessions on a positive upbeat note. End the lesson with an exercise both animal and child can do easily and then engage them in a play they can enjoy together. This will leave them feeling good about the training process and excited for future training sessions.

Don't push the child to train the animal for too long a time period. Ten to fifteen minutes for smaller pets and dogs is ample time. Horses will take a bit longer because of the exercise time required to get both the rider and the horse in shape. But even if the total riding time is thirty to forty-five minutes, only about fifteen to twenty should be spent in introducing and working on a new concept that is engaging the mental activity of both horse and rider. Ideally, any training session should end when both the animal and the child are excited and eager to continue. Entering and exiting training with a positive tone is of paramount importance for success.

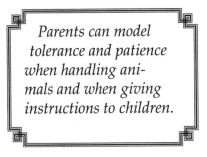

Parents can model tolerance and patience when handling animals and when giving instructions to children.

It takes time to create any successful relationship. Encourage your child to interact on a regular basis with his or her pet. To develop a silent communion with another being is magic. It strikes a primitive chord, resonating music deep within our soul.

Training time needs to be quality time and it must be scheduled into a day. It cannot be sandwiched between running to soccer practice and piano lessons. Interactions with the family pet (and your child) are as important as any other activity. It is impossible to teach an animal its lessons or to help a child gain tolerance and patience on a short timeframe. The time-crunched stress of our everyday lives is not conducive to developing relationships and opening communication.

If you plan to train your pet for fifteen minutes, schedule for thirty. Often you won't need the extra time but allowing for it promotes a relaxed atmosphere. This unhurried feeling is conducive for optimal interaction. You will be surprised how this relaxation will positively impact training sessions.

As a trainer, I often hear from parents that they feel they don't have enough time in their busy schedules to commit to three minutes let alone thirty. To this I reply that every single person on this earth enjoys the same twenty-four hours in each day. They have no more or no less. I believe that the difference between a time-stressed and a time-conscious person is his or her awareness of time and the choices he or she makes using each of these precious minutes. Consciously slowing down will help to make you aware of choices. It will help you take control.

- Christine Hamer

Sometimes it takes a bit of effort to persuade a child to live up to his commitment of the training and care of his pet. Although you should be sensitive to the age and maturity level of your child, it is important to help him or her to keep their commitment. Offer to help by working alongside the child. You may find this is an ideal time to talk about things that are going on at school or just to listen to whatever is on your child's mind. Sometimes it will be best to say nothing at all, just to feel the rhythm of the work and fall into a communal beat.

It is not enough simply to refill a water dish or place food out for your pet. In order for you and your child to reap the full value of sharing your life with another being, it is mandatory to become intimately involved in the relationship. The added value of inviting your pets to become an integral part of your life will reward your family with laughter and wonder.

"Although a child may experience many things in his world, none [is] so potent with information as the interaction with animals." (Becker) According to Marian Diamond in her book *Magic Trees of the Mind*, animals (and children) engaged in enriching activities stimulate growth in the cortex portion of the brain. She goes on to state that an important part of a child's intellect is developed kinesthetically, that is, by touch.

In order for children to develop their cognitive skills to the full potential, they must participate in a project, not just watch. Although this makes sense to most parents, consider the following facts: On any weekday, grade school children spend an average of more than two hours watching television (teenager averages are higher). On weekends that time increases by two and a half hours. Some studies suggest that television viewing may actually take up to four hours of each day for the typical child. By the age of eighteen, the average American child will have spent more of his or her life watching TV than any other single activity besides sleep. Since a child's kinesthetic ability is a part of his or her intelligence, the physical passivity inherent in TV viewing is harmful not only to the body but also to the mind.

Turn off the TV for an evening and turn on some quiet relaxing music. Your child can groom, stroke, or hold your pet while you read from a book, or vice versa. The family can sit and observe your pet or take a walk together and enjoy the abundance of nature, or write in your journal. Use this precious time to develop another relationship, the one between you and your child. Just as you have coached your child to pay attention to his pet, attend to your child. Look and listen with your heart.

"German Wire-haired Pointers. Good hunters. Ready early July."

"Maybe it's just some guys doing backyard breeding, but you might call," a breeder said to us when she didn't have any pups for sale.

So we did.

Chester, named after my Uncle Chet, was the runt. Bearded, long-legged, and scrawny, he was one of the last puppies and covered with tiny nip marks from his littermates. My husband did the New Puppy Tests: throw the ball, hide the ball, watch him with the other dogs. Chester was undeniable, always coming back, even when pounced on and pinned by the bigger pups. One way or another, he got the rag, the stick, or the ball. His spark and spirit, his tenacity jumped out as intense as his honey eyes.

We struck a deal with the breeder, and as we drove away, Richard said, "This dog has spunk. Besides, did you see those conditions? I wanted to rescue this dog."

I did too.

We registered him as "Chesterfield Smokes 'Em," and he began summer life of a Lake Dog with getting swimming lessons, retrieving balls, chasing ducks, and digging holes in my garden. He was in heaven. Summer turned to horseback riding and boating, house learning, and potty training. We were told this breed could seem hard-headed because the pointers learn quickly, and they don't want a lot of reminding. Sometimes, though, I couldn't tell if Chester was stubborn, being rebellious, or was confused. However, training seemed promising, even if it was a bit slower than with Bob, our Brittany.

When Chester was sixteen weeks, I started noticing some oddities. At first, we just thought it was his breed and his puppiness. He had developed a tremor. His head would shake from side to side when he looked at me, and his running seemed awkward, all legs and no coordination. In September, when the shaking became more pronounced, I took him to our vet.

"That's the weirdest thing I've every seen!" Lesley told me.

So she referred us to a doggie neurologist in Seattle. Clearly, we were the "parents of a special needs child." We were told that there were some scary and not-so-scary diagnoses, but to find out for sure what was wrong with him, it would cost a few thousand dollars, with no guarantee of rehabilitating him. So we made the hard decision to limit our spending.

We had some blood tests sent to the University of Pennsylvania Veterinarian School where researchers specialize in canine neurological disorders. They concluded that he had a Nonspecific Congenital Neurological condition that affected his gait, coordination, and vision. He would fall down and run

in an odd bunny-hop manner, back legs together as he jumped forward. He always seemed to think about his next move, sometimes for a very long time! But he wasn't in any pain.

Our neurologist told us there wasn't much data on his condition, but he might live a normal lifespan or wither away. "Most owners will put these dogs down once they are diagnosed. But you should be able to live pretty normally with him, so do what you usually do. He's lucky that he has you, and please, bring him in to see me any time. He's a sweet dog."

So we do our normal lives with him.

It is a warm day for a run, but we keep exercised and run on some river dikes with the dogs. Richard and Chester quickly move ahead while Bob and I run our slower, more steady pace.

At about two and a half miles, I am stopped by what I see: Chester is collapsed, panting and bawling.

Richard is standing passed him, watching, his face concerned.

"What's happened?" I rush to him.

"I don't know, but I think he's gotten over-heated. Let's get him to the water to cool down. He walks over to him and leads him on. Chester gets up when he sees me, takes a few steps and then falls down again. Up and forward one, two, flailing, falling-down steps, dragging his back legs behind him. Then a collapse, a woof, his eyes focused on us.

But Chester will not give up, so Richard encourages him on. Fifty more yards. We're unsure we're doing what's right, but know we need to learn Chester's limits and Chester learn his. Finally, Richard carries him to the drainage ditch and gently puts him in the water. He swims in circles, his back legs floating and flailing out to the side.

"I hope he doesn't drown," Richard says, as if reading my mind. Seconds later, he pulls him out and then, as if by magic, Shazam! Chester gets up and takes off like the starter gun just fired, beating us all back to the truck. Whaddaya know!

Weeks later as we run again together, watchers first giggle at his awkward gait. He looks like a rag doll, all floppy with eggbeater thawacka-thawacka footfalls. Then they see it.

"What's wrong with his legs? Was he hit by a car?"

"No, he's just like that, has been since birth."

"I feel bad. It's like laughing at someone who's handicapped."

"Don't worry. He's our spazzo dog. He makes us laugh all the time. And we love him all the more for it."

So, we don't have the hunting dog of our dreams or even a normal dog. What we do have is an inspiration. We marvel as he navigates his world. All of the traits we observed as a ten-week-old puppy, that tenacity that didn't keep him down after being bullied by his littermates, still runs strong. He is a constant reminder to us that we live the life we're given and it's up to us to put our heart and soul into making the most of it. As with much that comes our way, either as individuals or as parents, we get some surprises.

As I watch him struggle, my heart breaks, but I know it's something he needs to do. He has to find his own pace and limitations. So, as "parents of this special needs child," we learn the best situations for him and let him go. That's our job. He makes the most of it: living fully, making people smile, and devouring the world.

We made our choice, too. We let him be as normal as possible and take him on all of our adventures. Whether it's pheasant hunting or running on beaches, hiking in snow in the Cascades or fishing on the Columbia River, Chester is our adventure, our companion, our honey-eyed dancing dog.

-Molly Mcnulty
"Honey-eyed Dancing Dog"

PETS AND THE CIRCLE OF LIFE

"Animals help children learn to take care of others and also provide an extensive range of learning experiences. Sensitive issues like breeding and reproduction are approached more easily when animals are around to serve as object lessons. The wider the variety of animals, the greater the learning."

-Share Henry
Homeschooling the Middle Years

Where Do Babies Come From?

Children are curious about how life begins. "Where do babies come from?" is a question that makes some parents squirm. Birth can be introduced as part of the total lifecycle, the process of renewal, like spring growth in trees and flowers. Witnessing animals breed, using books to follow the development of the fetus, and then participating in the miraculous event of the animal giving birth can be growing experiences for both the parent and the child. The questions that arise quite naturally from this process should be answered "straight up" and without idioms. Children learn whether they can trust parents by the answers they are given. If a parent is honest, the child will continue to ask questions about life processes.

Both as a parent and as a nurse health educator in the public schools, I saw the positive effects of pets and animals on children's attitudes toward sexuality. For example, children in my health classes who had pets at home were not embarrassed with the subjects of reproduction and birth. They were excited to share their experiences. One child might tell about staying up late into the night to help his dog deliver a litter of puppies. The wonder of holding a new life in the palm of a hand was replayed for the whole class. Some of the children came from ranches where the selection and breeding of livestock was common conversation. These young people grew up accepting sexuality as a part of life. By relating these life processes to animals, even non-pet- owning classmates became more comfortable and were able to ask difficult questions.

- Margaret Hevel

At the seventh international conference on Human-Animal Interactions, Animals, Health and Quality of Life, S. Lookabaugh Triebenbacher, PhD, said, "A child who learns to care for an animal and treat it kindly and patiently, receives valuable training in learning to treat people the same way." Among the assets he listed that pets could provide for children were lessons about life, reproduction, birth, illnesses, death, and grieving.

> *When our youngest daughter was in high school, she loved going to the barn with her dad in the wee hours of the morning to watch the ewes give birth during lambing time. She said, "It was magic to me to witness something many other people don't have a chance to see. The quiet just before birth filled me with a beautiful peace."*

Children are constantly observing the behaviors of adults and of their own peers, trying to piece together the meaning behind people's words and actions. As parents, we are facilitators of learning, and therefore, our role should be to provide honest information. Beginning when our children are young, we should help them to feel good about themselves and about their bodies. According to Chrystal de Freitas, pediatrician and author of *Keys to Your Child's Healthy Sexuality*, "Children have a natural and healthy curiosity about all aspects of the world, including their body." The lessons about sexuality that a child learns during these formative years will either enhance their self image or thwart their personal growth. We teach by our attitude and by our behavior as much as by the words we say. Therefore, it is important for us to stop what we are doing to listen fully to what our child is trying to ask. Give them the attention they deserve for these very important (and for us sometimes difficult) questions. Our goal is to help children appreciate their individuality and guide them toward maturity.

Boys, Girls, and Sex

The topic of sex can evoke a myriad of feelings. The positive or negative emotions that parents may feel when they are talking about sex with their child will depend on the experiences that they had as a growing child. Many parents want to avoid "The Discussion, " yet human sexuality is the most important aspect of each child's personality development. It enables each individual to function as a male or female. Identifying who we are affects our view of the world.

The animal kingdom offers parents gender roles to use as examples when discussing male and female differences with their children. For example, in the lion kingdom, the lioness is the hunter. This can be compared to our society where men were the traditional providers. Today of course, the task of providing for the family is usually equally shared between both parenting partners. In birds of prey, the female is larger and stronger but it is still the male's duty to defend the territory and to provide for the female while she cares for the eggs. Since the expression of gender is constantly changing in today's world, we leave the discussion of what it means to be a man or a woman up to each individual family.

When children first ask questions about sexuality, responding simply with one or two sentences will usually quench their curiosity. At some point, however, parents may find the questions becoming uncomfortable. This may be the time to reflect upon your own personal feelings or perhaps unresolved issues. As we mentioned earlier, it is very important to pass unbiased facts to your child. If you find you are uncomfortable talking about sexuality, there are many resources available to help you communicate with your child. (See www.siecus.org, the Website of the Sexuality Information and Education Council of the United States.) If the idea of talking about sex makes you nervous, another option might be to direct your child's questions to a health care professional.

Sexual Development

As a child grows through each developmental stage, the changes in the body brings with it an awareness of his or her sexuality. Pets can be used in a positive role when discussing this delicate topic. Using animals to explain body parts and even the act of sex itself can provide a buffer between the parent and the uncomfortable subject. Often this will help a parent deal with this emotionally charged topic.

Infancy: As a parents love, cuddle, and talk to their newborn, the baby begins to feel good about him- or herself. The parents' acceptance of this unique person begins to foster feelings of self-worth. Talking about the body often begins as a game, where parents correctly name the baby's body parts. This very simple beginning has positive effects in helping the growing child become comfortable about his or her sexuality.

The family pet can assist with the child's expanding knowledge about body differences. Most children love to compare and to marvel at the differences and similarities between themselves and the pet. "Buffy has a tail but you don't have a tail! Look at Buffy's toes. Where are baby's toes?"

Preschool Years: Witnessing a loving relationship between parent caregivers is one of the components that help a child feel comfortable with his or her sexuality. It also creates a family atmosphere of love and trust. Hugs and kisses should be a part of daily life. But in order to do this effectively, parents will need to be comfortable with expressing emotions.

Preschoolers are rapidly developing their ability to express their opinions and ideas. Parents will need to be prepared in order to provide thoughtful answers to their young child's questions about sexuality. Simple and correct answers will build the child's confidence in the parent as a source of helpful information. Honesty will provide a trusting foundation and leave an open door for future questions. For example, viewing a nature program on TV may bring up the topic of mating. A parent may provide a simple, straightforward explanation such as "Mating is the way that animals make babies" or "When the girl lion knows it's time to have a baby (or is ready to be a mommy), she needs the boy lion to help make a baby lion."

When my children were young, part of my livelihood was the breeding of Labrador retrievers. We would raise about one litter a year as a part of our family. I was responsible for all of the parts of the process, including the actual breeding of the male and the female dogs. For those unfamiliar with the mating of canines, when the male enters the female, the male swells inside her, making what is called a tie. The two are, in essence, stuck together until the swelling recedes. On one such time, my four-year-old son came down and watched the process in silence. I was involved with the two dogs and didn't notice him standing there until the two dogs had tied. I made sure that they were standing quietly so as not to injure each other. Then I turned and saw my son. I wondered what he was thinking, but before I could ask, he inquired about what they were doing. I told him that they were ready to make some puppies and this is how it is done. I was prepared to give a further, more in-depth explanation, but this seemed to be enough. "Oh," he said, "I guess they look like they're having fun." With this he walked off to play.

Early School Years: At the end of a school day, many children walk or bike home with friends. Or they may ride the school bus, always filled with lively chatter. During this time, children will talk about every topic with each other, including sex. Sometimes they will pass on misinformation, tales, and folklore as fact. At such times, your child may return home with questions about what was said. Whatever issues may arise as a result of these questions, an understanding parent will listen and encourage the child to talk about how this made him or her feel. Some of the stories your child may tell will seem outrageous, but don't laugh. This is especially true if the misinformation came from a close friend. To dismiss a false statement as silly is the same as calling the child's friend silly and therefore your child as well because he or she believed what the friend said. Your child is placing a huge amount of trust in you to handle these questions gently.

Children don't understand the sex act in the adult sense. However, they are able to understand about how life begins. The idea that a fertilized egg can grow into a special animal or person is marvelous to them. As a result, a child may ask more specific questions on creation such as "How did I get in your stomach?" or "How did I get out of your tummy?" This is where animals can be wonderful examples to help a child learn about reproduction and birth. Children raised on a farm or ranch have an opportunity to see the natural breeding and birth process of a variety of animals. For families in metropolitan areas, a trip to a zoo or farm can be a classroom for learning about life cycles. The beauty and wonder of new life can be talked about as children watch animals care for their young. Personnel at a zoo maternity ward can provide additional information to both parent and child.

Often children between the ages of five and eight begin to develop a sense of modesty. They may want to take a bath by themselves or perhaps shut their bedroom door while dressing. Children deserve the right to manage their own bodies as they develop. Parents can acknowledge this need with caring, supportive words. "I understand that you would like to dress yourself. If you need help, let me know."

Adolescence: The preteen years can be anxious ones because of the major physical changes that the child is undergoing. Parents need to reassure the young person that the changes in his or her body are are perfectly normal and a sign of becoming an adult. The preteen may have more questions about sex and about fetal development. Because preteens are so sophisticated these days, parents should not assume what their child may  or may not know about sex. It is important for the parents to initiate the conversation and delicately to assess what gaps may exist in their child's education. Sexual themes are constantly appearing in movies, magazines, and television. Sometimes these images provide false information. Therefore, it is important that parents correct this and to clarify the positive values about sexuality. Talking about sex with your preteen will help the child to establish morals that will lead to responsible choices. Therefore, it is important for parents to take the time needed for their preteen to become comfortable with sexuality. When parents understand and talk with their child about the child's blossoming feelings, they will insure their child's positive self-image as an adult.

Young Adult: A parent's primary job is to guide the teenager through the adult choices and the difficult issues of drugs, alcohol, tobacco, and sexual relationships. In addition to handling these adult demands, the teen has to cope with the pressures of school and friends.

Adolescence is designed by nature to put a wedge between parent and child. This sets the stage to insure that both can let go when it's time for the teen to be on his or her own. Because of this natural separation process, the family pet can often offer something parents cannot provide. There will be days when the teenager wishes he or she were a young child again without responsibilities, a time when Mom and Dad made all of the decisions and took care of everything. The teen may want to return to the time when all he or she had to do was play and have fun. In searching for comfort, the teen will not think it's okay to play with toys from childhood. However, it is okay to hang out with a furry playmate from youth. The family pet may provide stability at a time when the world seems topsy-turvy.

As parents, we hope that by the time our child has grown into the teenage years, he or she will have learned the basic morals and values that are important to our family. Often abstinence is one of these values. It is difficult when our teen makes choices that conflict with our beliefs. This is all part of the stretch to reach individuality. It does not help for us to lecture or to threaten the teen to follow our value system. Rather than altering the teenager's opinion, we will only alienate the young person we are trying to help. The resulting rebellion will only become stronger with each emotional reaction received from the parents. Instead, this is a perfect time to ask questions such as "Why do you believe this?" or "What makes you feel this way?" Truly caring and trying to understand the teen's point of view will make the most impact on a rebellious teen. Above all, when the whole world seems uncertain, teens need to know their parents believe and trust in them. More than any other time, this is the point where we need to reflect on what our pets teach us daily, the art of unconditional love.

Baby Chicks in My Classroom

Styrofoam and RUSH.
You came as a birthday surprise
From a mail order catalog in Kansas.
Tiny eggs ready for my incubator,
Ready to be amazing.
And you were:
I couldn't keep those awkward teenage boys away
And didn't want to.
Jessie raced in each morning
Hoping.
Twenty-four
Assorted Bantam eggs.
Moisture levels checked,
Recorded.
Three daily turnings
So you wouldn't stick to your shell.
Then one day,
Twenty-one later
Jessie's ear to the box
"I can hear them!!"
We watched you be born.
We cheered you on.
We held you as you unfolded in our hands.
You were so ugly:
Slimy—all head, eyes, and feet.
A dozen little lives: yellows and blacks and almost whites.
Everyone wanted to hold you
And give you names:
Mohawk, Bo Peep, Fred.
Forever changing our lives.

-Molly McNulty

GRIEF

To everything there is a season . . . a time to be born and a time to die.

- Ecclesiastes 3: 1-2

Birth and death are the twin sisters of mortality, the very mysteries of life. To a doctor, these words define clinical processes. But to someone whose heart has been opened by the joy of birth or the grief of loss, these words are very personal. They exemplify the welcome of new life or the exit of a life that they hold dear.

Like a great artist, the seasons display the life cycle. The theme is painted in repeating patterns and colors. Spring, summer, fall, and winter. Birth, youth, maturing, and death.

Death is painful. With few exceptions, the human lifespan is longer than other animals with which we share the planet. As a result, we are witness to many revolutions of the life wheel. And because of this, we become practiced at grief. Children experience this life process questioning "How? Why?" and not only the why of death but, more important, also the why of the pain associated with loss.

The emotions of sorrow and of fear that arise from the death of a pet can put us in touch with our own mortality. Experiencing the death of a loved one is a journey. Each individual travels this road in his or her own way and time. As parents, we can share our experiences with our children and hope that they will hear a resonating note. The death of a family pet leaves both children and adults feeling helpless and lost. How a parent approaches the subject of death will depend on the age of the child.

Very young children do not understand the permanency of death. It seems to them as though the person or pet has gone on a trip.

Lemon was a beautiful orange speckled English setter. She loved coming to work with me and helped a great deal as I molded young dogs into successful hunting partners for their owners. Although she enjoyed her job at the kennel, her life was incomplete until she met my youngest son. She loved Nathan from the time I brought him home from the hospital. When he began to toddle around the house, she was always with him. It was not uncommon to find him asleep on the back porch curled close to Lemon. He would take his blankets to her bed and bundle the two of them as one.

They would walk together through the house, Nathan's tiny arm locked around the setter's neck. During cartoon time, she was his pillow. In his playroom, she was a part of the scene for his toys. The two were inseparable.

The language of toddler is not articulate, and understanding them is a challenge, even for their parents. Although I couldn't always understand what Nathan said to Lemon, she seemed to comprehend every word. Their communication was miraculous. People search a lifetime to find the kind of reciprocal love and devotion the two shared. They were kindred spirits.

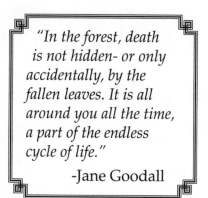

"In the forest, death is not hidden- or only accidentally, by the fallen leaves. It is all around you all the time, a part of the endless cycle of life."

-Jane Goodall

In the spring of Lemon's ninth year, she became slower, quite out of character. She still happily wagged her tail at our approach, but her eyes were duller. Even Nathan, who was just a little over two, noticed the difference. He would push her food close so she wouldn't have to rise from her bed to eat and would cover her with one of his special blankets for the night. It didn't help; she still lost weight.

I drove her to the vet, fearing the worst. My nightmare was confirmed, cancer. The sorrow of impending loss choked my throat and flooded my eyes. It dropped as tears on the orange and white dog with the large brown eyes. I brought her home with the vet's assurance that she was in no pain. About two weeks later, Lemon's breathing became labored. I stroked her ears and told her it would end soon. I called Tom with the news, barely able to speak. We made our plans to say goodbye and to put her at peace that evening. I cried that day, that night, and the next day. We all felt incredible grief, but the worst ache was explaining what was happening to Nathan. Though he nodded his small head and said he understood, we knew it was more than a two-and-a-half-year-old mind could comprehend. For months he would ask, "Where's Lemon?" and we would reply that she had died. At first he would exclaim, "She's dead?" then cry as if she had just died at that moment in his arms. We would hold and comfort him, shedding more tears ourselves. Time passed, and though he continued to ask, "Where's Lemon," he then would respond with the wooden expression, "Oh, Lemon's dead," as if it were a sad poem and not a truth in his life.

Lemon's special gift to Nathan will last a lifetime. He has a deep empathy for animals and an ability to communicate with them that borders on telepathy. He is especially fond of white dogs with light orange speckling. She gave unconditionally and was always happy. Powerful lessons. I feel privileged to have shared her time on earth. She was one in a million, the kind of dog that legends are made of.

- Christine Hamer

As children mature, they begin to understand that there is a beginning and ending to life. Nearing the age of ten, the child is ready to understand Elliot Kranzler's four attributes of death.

1. Death has an exact cause.

2. Death involves the end of life.

3. Death is irreversible.

4. Death is worldwide.

At this time, children may ask about death as it relates to both people and animals. "How does it feel to die?" and "What happens after death?" are common questions. A dead chipmunk or bird found on a walk, the way that plants change with the seasons, or the death of a family pet are all opportunities for a child to learn that death is the end of life.

Depending upon the family's religion, the child may inquire if animals have a soul. In her article, "Do Animals Have Souls?" Dr. Aurelia Louise Jones wrote, "This is a controversial subject, and I leave it up to you to decide. Many believe everything in the universe is consciousness and life. St. Francis of Assisi in his time knew this to be true. In January 1990, Pope John Paul II issued a proclamation declaring that animals have souls." Dr. Jones closes with Bible references from Genesis, a section she feels supports the idea that animals have souls.

"Children can't understand the permanence of death until they're about ten years old. And most of them don't carry emotional baggage about the sadness of death like adults do. They just want to know the facts."

-Jean Faull, Child-development and behavior specialist

And God created great whales, and every living creature that moveth, which the waters brought forth abundantly, after their kind, and every winged fowl after their kind: and God saw that it was good.

And God said, "Let the earth bring forth the living creature
after his kind, cattle, and every thing that creepeth upon the
earth after his kind: and God saw that it was good."

-Genesis 1: 21, 24

Death can be stressful. It is best to explain as much as the
child can understand as soon as possible to avoid misconception.
Children know when something's wrong. They watch our actions

and overhear bits and pieces
of conversation. They may
witness visitors talking with
us in low voices. It is important that parents take the time
to talk about the changes that
are occurring in the house and
their own emotions. Anything
that disrupts children's familiar routines and their feelings
of safety can toss them into
turmoil. If parents can keep
a steady household routine
it will help the child to feel
more secure.

Although some children may react to loss with feelings of
grief, others may not find the incident upsetting. Whatever your
child feels or doesn't feel is okay. For example, children of all ages
need to know that crying is okay. In fact, it is necessary to help
them through the pain of loss. They also need to know that there
is nothing wrong with them if they don't feel like crying.

When a child's pet companion dies, emotional chaos may follow. One minute the child may want to be alone while the next
minute he or she may be clinging to your leg, needing your comfort. Invariably your child will ask "Why. . .?" Children aren't really
expecting an answer about the death, but rather, they are looking

for a way to ease their hurt. We need to let our children know they have permission to talk about death. Children will feel that their mixed-up feelings are valid when parents take time to listen.

Along with wondering why, a child may be filled with guilt, believing he or she might be the cause of the tragedy. For example, the child may wonder if the pet died because he or she forgot to feed it or may think "If I hadn't been mean to my dog, he wouldn't have died." Parents need to tell their child that he or she had nothing to do with the pet's death, explaining the cause as clearly and simply as they can. Parents can also provide caring messages such as "Pete loved you. Remember how he curled up on your pillow each night? We were so lucky to have shared our lives with a special kitty like Pete."

When a child's world turns upside down, emotions of fear, guilt, and anger can create disruptive behaviors. The love and acceptance that is offered by pets can provide a safe place for children to recover from hurt.

In one of the health classes I taught in an elementary school, my students were all hearing impaired. Billie had the trauma of a divorce in his family plus the death of a grandparent, all within a month's time. He began acting up in class and at home. I knew that when we are unable to communicate our feelings proactively, they often emerge in less acceptable ways. As hurt accumulates, people shut down.

One day I brought one of our spring lambs for the students to see. After petting time and talking about farm animals, I put the lamb in a small enclosure and continued with class. I watched Billie gravitate to the lamb and signed to the others to leave him alone. Billie lay down next to the lamb and stroked her softly. That afternoon he finished his work without bothering his classmates. I borrowed a rabbit from another classroom for the next few weeks and had Billie help with the care of this bunny. At a conference with his mother, she said that Billie's behavior

at home had improved. He had stopped the unexplained crying
and hitting of his sister. Pets do indeed help to heal.

- Margaret Hevel

When talking with our children about death, it doesn't help to beat around the bush, thinking this will ease the pain. For example, rather than saying something such as "Spade had an accident this morning. Someone opened the backyard gate, and he ran out, and was hit by a car." It is better for the parent to make the simple honest statement, "Spade died this morning." You can fill in the appropriate details later if

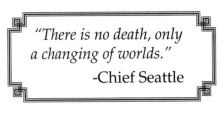

"There is no death, only a changing of worlds."

-Chief Seattle

the child asks. Being straightforward doesn't have to appear cold and unfeeling. Your caring will come through in the understanding tone of your voice.

It is important for parents to assure their child that, although the physical body has died, the love that they feel for that person or animal will live on. This might be explained something like, "Grandfather has died, but that doesn't mean we don't still love him. We will carry this love and his memory forever in our hearts."

It's helpful for parents to be familiar with the process of grieving. "If a person is old enough to love, he or she is old enough to grieve," says Naomi Matthews, Program Manager for a children's grieving program at St. John's Health System in Detroit. The five stages of grief are: denial, anger, bargaining, depression, and finally, acceptance. Adults and children don't move through these stages at the same pace. Children generally handle grief more gracefully than adults. However, parents need to be watchful for signs that their child might be having difficulty with one of the stages. Understanding this process will help parents identify where their child may be struggling.

For instance, if a child is experiencing anger, the second stage in the grieving process, it can sometimes appear in the form of aggressive behavior.

"These are not my things! Get your stuff out of my room!" Jim slammed his bedroom door, closing out the pile of discarded clothes and toys. Mother motioned the younger boy away from the pile and the door. "It's okay," she mouthed. She looked at the pile. Among the toys and clothes belonging to her younger son was Nellie's blanket and favorite toy. Nellie had died yesterday after being struck by a car. The ache was still raw, and she imagined Jim was feeling the same. Quietly she knocked on the door and then opened it. "Jim?"

Jim was lying on the bed, pillows piled over his head. At seventeen, he was pretty good at ignoring adults when he really wanted. Right now he wanted the whole world to go away. His mother sat on the bed, removed the top pillow and brushed the brown curls from Jim's face.

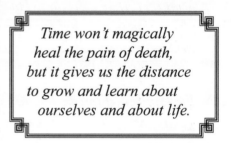

Time won't magically heal the pain of death, but it gives us the distance to grow and learn about ourselves and about life.

"Honey, I know you're hurting inside. I miss Nellie, too."

"I don't miss that stupid ole dog." Jim's voice was muffled, but his mother still felt the pain. "She was too stupid to stay away from that car." Then quieter still, "I was too stupid to know how to stop her."

Mother gathered her lanky teen into her arms, his head draped on her shoulders, the bulk of his body stretched out on the bed. "Remember when you were small enough for me to hold all of you on my lap? Now look at you." She continued to stroke his head. "Honey, you can't blame yourself or Nellie for the accident. Being angry for something that will not change helps no one. Not Nellie and certainly not you. I know you loved Nellie; she slept right here beside your bed every night. What you're feeling right now hurts, but it will get better."

"But it aches deep inside. I've never had anything hurt so bad." Jim turned his face toward his mother, tears ready to fall.

"I know it does. It hurts real bad. But this is natural. It's okay to feel sorrow when we experience a loss. It's okay to grieve when someone dies. Sometimes part of that grieving process is being angry, and that's okay, too, as long as we don't get stuck in our anger. All of this is part of learning to be human, learning to be a man." She gave her son a kiss. "I have an idea. Sometimes it helps to ease the sorrow when we talk about the person or animal that we've lost. How about if I go and get Nellie's photo album? We could look at the pictures of her as a puppy. Remember when she would grab the blanket off your bed and run around the house with it in her mouth?"

Jim smiled through his tears. "Yeah. She loved that blanket so much we ended up giving it to her for keeps." Jim sat up and looked at his mother. "I'm sorry I yelled. I was sore at Nellie and angry that I couldn't save her. I think talking about her helps. I'll go get her album."

> Understanding death and grieving helps us to be less fearful about this natural life process every living thing will experience.

It is important for parents to continue to offer support to their child by telling him or her that they understand what the child is feeling. They can help the child explore why he or she feels angry and explain that whatever the emotion, it's a natural part of grieving for someone we love.

How parents behave rather than the words they use will be a greater influence on whether a child accepts or fears death. Physical comfort is an important part of the healing process. When the death is of a member of the family or a close friend or another animal, the steady presence of the family pet during this stressful time can be a great help, especially to children. The animal's company allows the child to transfer the love that he or she can no longer give to the one that has died. Adults sometimes interrupt or attempt to censor the pain that pours from a child's heart. However a pet will feel a child's anger and or sorrow without judgment. It can provide the benefit of additional physical comfort when the child holds it in the hand or lap or puts an arm around its neck. The slow rhythmic breathing of an animal can relieve the tension of stress for all ages.

Dave Walton, nicknamed Wally, began his love affair with the helicopter when he signed up for military flying. After the service, he flew the helicopter for the Forest Service. While working as a member of the fire crew, we met, fell in love, and married in 1990.

For three winters, Dave and I worked at Ruby Mountain in Elko, Nevada. He was a pilot for the Heliski trips while I dispatched. One day, a winter storm delayed the crew's departure. Dave and his clients waited an hour before takeoff. Three minutes into the flight, the helicopter crashed. I was devastated. There are no words for the agonizing emptiness that clouded my mind and soul. The painful loss blackened my day and invaded the darkness of night to haunt my dreams of what used to be and could never be again.

"We need to get Linda a puppy," my friend's ten-year-old daughter, Jo, said.

I said I wasn't interested.

"Just come with me and take a look," she insisted.

So, I did. They were sweet but I didn't need a puppy. I wouldn't even know how to care for one.

I left for a week on the river. On the second day of my return, I put my cat kennel in the car before leaving to town. "I'm not going to get a dog. I don't have a clue what to do with a pup," on the way I murmured, "but if I did get a dog, I'd name him Wally." Of course, Wally came home.

Two weeks later, somehow Wally slipped out of the yard. I was on the phone when I heard the knock on the door. I opened it to a man. The expression on his face made my heart jump. My thoughts collided. Wally . . . where's Wally? . . . I need him . . . Please don't let him be hurt . . .I need him!

As if from a faraway tunnel, the words echoed. "Do you have a white dog? Ma'am, do you have a white dog?"

"Oh no---ooo!"

"I think I hit him."

I ran past the man, down the steps. . . . "Wally! Wally!" I found him under the porch covered with blood. Tears ran. My mind swirled. Not you too. Don't you die on me . . . please, Wally–don't die on me! Gently, I lifted him and drove to the vet.

An angel smiled on Wally and on me that day. No doctor's prescription could have lifted my grief and healed my soul like the one small dog named Wally.

Wally is now eleven years old. I will always be grateful for the gift a little dog named Wally gave me at a time when my life was filled with pain and loneliness. He found and touched my aching heart with his unconditional love.

Elementary school aged children understand the finality of death. They may ask about the circumstances surrounding a pet's death. They may worry about their own health or that of other family members. It is natural for children to question all mortality: "Mac died. Will I die tomorrow? Will Mommy die?" Parents can address these fears by giving a straightforward answer, "We will all die someday, but I hope to live a long time, and I think you will too."

Preteens and adolescents may ask for details of how the body changes with death. They may want to know the exact process and the biology of how the body dies. It is not uncommon for the teen to experience physical symptoms with the intense grief of loss. Such physical manifestations

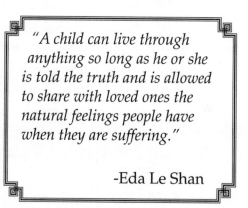

"A child can live through anything so long as he or she is told the truth and is allowed to share with loved ones the natural feelings people have when they are suffering."

-Eda Le Shan

might be loss of appetite, trouble sleeping, mood swings, complaints of stomachaches, or headaches.

As with younger children, a pet can help the teen through the grieving transitions. The animal's presence and "listening ear" may allow the teen to express his or her feelings during a time when he or she may not be able to tell a parent. Stroking the warm fur of a kitty or dog or laughing at the playful antics of the hamster can all help the teen to regain balance.

Healing

One approach to begin the healing process is to consider all of life a gift. Parents can illustrate this concept by explaining that some gifts are permanent, such as the beauty of the sky, and others are fragile and cannot last forever, such as our pets. Exactly what is said about the spiritual side of death will depend on each family's religious beliefs.

A funeral honors the life of the person or animal that has died. This ceremony may bring closure for children just as it may for adults. However, children can have scary thoughts about the unknown experience of a funeral. Words such as dying, funeral, casket, and cemetery are cloaked in a dark mystery that often weaves the element of fear in many children. Their vivid imaginations can take them into frightening nightmares. Understanding what it means to pay last respects to a loved one and why we practice various rituals associated with saying goodbye will all be helpful to our children. Helping your child feel a part of your cultural traditions is important. Your child can be encouraged but should not be forced to attend a memorial or funeral service.

When a beloved pet dies, working on a memorial will help the healing process. Below we have suggested some healing activities for parents and their child to do together.

1) Write a letter to the pet saying all of the things you want it to know. This note can be tucked away, buried with the pet, or burned symbolically to carry the message toward heaven.

2) Create a scrapbook about the life of your pet. It can be filled with pictures, stories, and special items. Young people of all ages enjoy the memory of photographs. Looking through a photo album can provide a wonderful opportunity for both parents and children to recall the special times they spent with their pet. "Look . . . this is you showing your rabbit, Cedar, at the fair. You got a blue ribbon that summer. Here you are feeding him the fresh hay Grandpa brought from the ranch. And here you are holding him. Remember how you laughed when he tickled your nose while you hugged him close?" Don't be afraid to laugh, even during the sad times. Humor during a time of sorrow helps to affirm life. The moment of joy will honor the pet that has died.

3) A memorial service can provide an opportunity for children to release their emotions and allow the healing process to begin. It also lets parents teach their beliefs about what happens after death. Perhaps it is appropriate to bury the beloved pet in the flower or vegetable garden. A box lined with a soft cloth can hold the pet. Sometimes children want to tuck in their pet's favorite toy. "Pete needs this to play with in heaven." Planting a beautiful perennial flower can be a long-lasting memorial to a wonderful life.

As adults, we are often still sorting through our own feelings and beliefs regarding mortality. It's okay to tell our children, "I don't know the answer to your question. I'm still trying to figure this out myself. How about if we look together for the answer?" Your answer may come "from the mouth of babes." To help you in your quest, we have listed some resources on coping with death at the end of the book.

THE COMMUNICATION BRIDGE

Notice to the children of the McKinney family:
Story-time is at 7:30 PM. All children who are in their PJ's with
teeth brushed are invited.
-Love, Mom & Dad

We communicate by speaking, by writing words, by giving facial expressions, and by making gestures. These are the ways we convey our feelings, share information, and impart knowledge to others. But the process is not simple. Language can be interpreted in a variety of ways. Although the speaker may have a clear thought in his mind, the receiver may come to a different interpretation. The result can be frustrating for both. In fact, when one thinks about the number of misconceptions that could arise while attempting to communicate with others, it's a wonder we are able to relate effectively at all.

Communication can be difficult between parents and children. Children can find communication especially frustrating when they are trying to express feelings but don't yet have a full grasp of language.

As parents, we can open or close communication with our children by the words we choose. It is best if we choose phrases that invite the child to speak more about what is on his or her mind. For example, "You look worried" or "I'm not sure I understand what you're trying to tell me. Do you mean . . .?" are all ways to open the door, inviting the child to speak more.

Whereas when we use phrases such as "That's stupid" or "Don't be ridiculous" or "Oh, come on now!" we close the door to future interaction.

Words are weighted with emotion, and the ones that we choose can either bruise our children's fragile personality or become a hug to their heart.

As parents, we need not only to communicate our needs and thoughts but also to understand our child's desires and feelings. The words we choose to communicate our ideas can either create strife or invite harmony. Talking *to* our child only signals our needs: This is how I want things done. As a result, our child will feel powerless and will resent what he or she feels is our attempt at control. However when parents talk *with* their child, it opens the door to a cooperative approach. It conveys the message that the parent wants the child to have a creative role in the outcome. When parents take the time to listen to their child about what they are thinking and how they are feeling and then to share their own thoughts and feelings, more positive communication is inevitable.

> *Another way we can help young children gain self-confidence is to empower them by giving them choices.*

Young preschool aged children are teetering between babyhood and childhood. This is a time when they still need our care but they are sprouting the shoots of individuality. Offering choices will help to give the preschooler some control over his or her life and to communicate, "I'm confident you can help take care of yourself." However, for this to be successful, parents must be willing to live with the child's decision. Asking a question such as "Do you want to put your coat on now to go outside?" invites the potential for the child to answer "No. " Often a coat is needed, and not wearing one is really not an option. One way parents can eliminate the potential for a negative response is by choosing their words carefully. Instead, offer the child a concrete choice. "Would you like to wear your red coat or the blue one this morning?"

Older children, can be encouraged to examine the outcome of their choices if parents ask questions such as "What do you think will happen if you . . .?" or "How will you feel about this?"

The gerbil was out of water, again. Mary's mother could feel her frustration rising. She had asked Mary to check on her pet's water just an hour ago. Her inclination was to let Mary know in not uncertain terms how she felt about this recurring problem. However, she took a few minutes and a deep breath to regain her composure. Then she went into Mary's room where she found her daughter fully engaged in a video game.

"Mary, I need you to put the game on pause for a minute." Mary didn't seem to hear her mother, so she stepped in front of the picture. This seemed to break the trance. "Mary, please place the game on pause so that we can talk." Mary did as her mother asked. Mary's mother took her daughter by the hand and led her into the family room where the thirsty gerbil was nibbling at some apple bits.

"Can you tell me why we're in here?" Mary's mother asked.

"Oh, because I forgot to give Squeaky some water this morning?" Mary answered.

"That's right. When you get thirsty, what do you do?"

"I go into the kitchen and pour myself some juice."

"What do you suppose would happen if you went to the kitchen but there was no juice in the refrigerator because I forgot to go to the store?"

Mary hung her head and mumbled, fully aware of where her mother was going with this conversation, "I'd go thirsty."

"That's right. It's my responsibility to make sure that you always have something to eat and to drink, and it's your responsibility to Squeaky that he is cared for in the same fashion. I want you to fill up Squeaky's water right now and to make sure that he has plenty of fresh food. I know that you like to play video games when you have finished your school work, but Squeaky's care has to come first. What can we do to help you remember?"

Mary's face lit with her idea," How 'bout we put a note on my video game that says 'Squeaky needs water!'"

"That's a wonderful idea. That's something you're bound to see. Right after you take care of Squeaky, let's make the note, tape it to your game, and then you can go back to playing. That sound ok?"

Mary nodded her head.

Children thrive on approval. Feelings of success or failure are promoted by our words.

Our children need the chance to talk about the big and the little things that happen throughout their day. If we keep an open heart, we will find that they are often relieved that we are there to listen to their uncomfortable feelings: "I didn't think you'd understand." or "I'm glad I could tell you."

"Hi honey, how was school today?" Billy's mom set out the snack on the kitchen table as her youngest son walked through the door. He was dragging his backpack, a sure sign that the day hadn't gone well. She knew that Billy was struggling with some of his studies and that reading especially was difficult for him.

"At school, during reading, my words came out all wrong. Everyone laughed at me. "

Billy's mother went to her son and took the backpack from his hand. She gave her son a hug and a kiss and then walked with him over to the kitchen table, her arm around his shoulders.

"You must have felt terrible. Reading is hard work. It takes practice just like when you learned how to ride your bike. You practiced over and over until you rode smoothly."

"Yeah, but that was easy. Reading is hard," Billy said, taking a bite of the sandwich his mother had set out.

"Yes, learning to ride the bike was an easy activity for you, but not all children can learn that easily. I had a very hard time learning to ride a bike, but now I can ride well. Reading is just like learning to ride a bike. You start out slow and careful with someone watching over your shoulder to catch you if you fall. Then you read a little faster."

Billy's eyes brightened. "And you'll have to run to keep up with me."

His mother laughed, "That's right, and then soon after, you'll be reading all on your own. All you have to do is practice reading the words until they come smoothly. You know who loves to hear stories? Buffy. I just know that she would love to hear you read."

Billy looked down and considered the little cocker at his feet. When she saw that Billy was looking at her, she began to wag her tail. "She won't laugh at me when I get the words wrong, huh."

"You're right. Buffy likes anything that you can read. After your snack, why don't you go and get your book. Buffy will curl up with us on the couch. I'll help you with the words."

Communication is more than using words. Nonverbal communication comes in many forms. For example, we clap, hit, shove, kick, cry, and laugh. We touch, hug, and kiss. Body language tells others how we feel. We may pout, frown, slump, smile, or clench our fists. Understanding nonverbal language is an important social skill that will help our children to interact with and to acquire friends more easily. The ability to read nonverbal communication helps children to interpret correctly what is being said. In *Animals and Children*, Bob Christiansen explains, "Animals are helpful for increasing social and verbal interaction and appear to improve a child's mastery of nonverbal communication."

> *Children from pet owning families are better at reading and understanding facial expressions and body language than those from non-pet households.*
>
> -Bob Christiansen

We have all heard the expression that actions speak louder than words. We tend to believe what we see rather than what we hear. A smile or lack thereof can distinguish between a joke and an insult. Concern and warmth in the eyes of a parent and the gentle inflection in the voice adds a layer of meaning to the casual words "How are you?"

One powerful form of nonverbal communication is touch. An arm across our child's shoulders or a hug conveys comfort and the message, "I love you." Touch is a powerful tool that can penetrate barriers where words will not. Petting a family pet is therapeutic for the pet and for the person. When a child is upset, interacting with the pet can help both of them to relax.

Dave noticed that his five-year-old daughter was becoming frustrated with her project. Before the situation got out of hand, he walked over to their black Lab, Lady, who was resting on the living room rug.

"Sarah, I need your help with Lady." Lady thumped her tail in response to Dave's voice but didn't lift her head. Dave knew Sarah loved Lady and was always concerned about her happiness.

"What's wrong with her?" Sarah asked as she joined her father on the rug.

"I'm not sure; she just seems a little upset. I have an idea how we can make her feel better, but I'll need your help too. Sit down next to her and take a deep breath."

Sarah and Dave both took a deep breath.

"Good," Dave said. "Now, take your hands like this." Dave took his daughter's hands in his own and began to work on the dog's shoulder. "And massage her shoulder like this. Good, now slower. And we need to breathe deep to help her relax." Dave and Sarah took another deep breath, and Dave slowed his strokes even further.

"Look how she is relaxing. Watch how her chest rises more slowly. She has closed her eyes. Lady feels better already. Would you like to rest for a few minutes like Lady? I could rub your back."

A great way to teach about nonverbal communication is by referring to the family pet. An animal's main form of communication is with body posturing and subtle facial, ear, and tail signals. Helping children to learn how to understand a pet's way of communication also keeps both the child and the pet safe. For example, young children are often unaware of the signs that they may be in trouble with the family pet. Therefore, it is important for parents to take the time to explain what the pet's behavior is telling the child. Pets that have been raised with children are generally tolerant of their unpredictable behavior. However there will be times when even they have had enough. Children should be taught to respect an animal's need for quiet time. If a young child tries to lie with the family cat and the cat gets up and walks away, this is a perfect opportunity to explain what the cat is saying without words. "When Socks walks away from you, she's telling you that she wants to rest by herself for a while. We need to make sure that Socks gets her rest time when she needs it."

A child's ability to correctly read a pet's communication signals will help to prevent accidents and injuries. Other examples a parent might give of a cat's nonverbal behavior could be "If the kitty's tail bristles and she gives a low growl, she is saying 'Don't touch me.'" or "When Muffin's ears are lying flat against her head, she is telling you to leave her alone" or "When kitty bumps against your arm or leg, it probably means, 'I'm happy to see you; let's play' or maybe 'Pet me.'" Even if a parent believes the child understands the pet's body language, it is still imperative to monitor all interactions between the child and the family pet. (For more information about animal communication, see the chapter "Pets Teach Tolerance" and the resources at the end of the book.)

Misbehavior = Miscommunication

Both children and animals let us know what their needs are by the way they behave. Behaviors are an outward reflection of an inward flow of emotions. We label some of these behaviors as acceptable, some not. From a parent's perspective, misbehavior equals a problem for the parent. As parents, we are often stressed from the ups and downs of daily life, and therefore, we may fail to look for the undercurrent, that is, the cause of our child's behavior. It helps to look at misbehavior as miscommunication. We forget that our child is attempting to tell us something by his or her actions, or we may misread what our child is trying to say. When this happens, both the child and the parent become frustrated from the inadequate communication. The child's behavior generally becomes more pronounced, a form of shouting in an attempt to get the parent to hear what is being said. Instead of allowing the outcome of this situation to spin out of control, we can direct the circumstance by trying to understand what the child's behavior is struggling to tell us. One way to improve this communication is to help our children alter their behavior, by showing them a better way to express their needs.

Mother and Suzie have been running errands all day. Mother is in a hurry. The grocery store is her last stop before going home. "I want a cookie," Suzie says. Mother's thinking about what she'll fix for dinner when she says, "You can't have one now; it's too close to dinner." Suzie slumps down in the middle of the isle. "I want a cookie! I want a cookie!" Mother only sees the embarrassing and unacceptable behavior. But Suzie is trying to tell her mother that she's tired of waiting and needs to go home. Before Suzie's meltdown, mother had an option. She could have said something such as "I understand that you're tired and hungry. We're almost done shopping, and then we will go home. Why don't you pick out a special cookie to take home for dessert?"

Mother also can talk with Suzie about her behavior by using language that reflects the positive aspects of her daughter's words and actions rather than the negative ones. *"Suzie, I'm so proud of how patient you have been all day. I know that it's hard to do all of this shopping. We deserve a treat don't you think? I'll tell you what; we need something for dessert tonight, how about if you pick it out?"*

Note that this is not done as a means to control the child's behavior or as a bribe to obtain good behavior. Surprise rewards for exemplary behavior are perfectly acceptable.

Just like our children, when the family pet misbehaves, it is trying to tell us something through its actions. We can use this incident not only to explain the animal's behavior to the child but also as a way to help our children to learn about appropriate ways to use words rather than actions to get what they want.

For instance, it is common for a young energetic pup to jump on a child. Rather than merely chastising the ignorant pup, a wise parent can turn this into a lesson. Picking the child up, a parent might say something such as "Puppy pushed you down because he wanted to play with you. But we know pushing someone is not acceptable behavior. It hurts. Instead of pushing your friend, what would you do?" The child might answer, "I'd say, 'Mary, can I play with that now?'"

"That's a good way to ask. Let's teach our puppy a better way to ask to play with us. You can help. We'll show him how he can get our attention by sitting quietly in front of us. Then we can give him what he wants, praise and pats."

As our children move through the different growth and development stages, we will face periods of misbehavior (or miscommunication). From a parent's point of view, their antics sometimes appear as outright defiance toward family values and the rules of proper conduct. Helping our children to make the proper choices can be stressful for parents. A child's consistent whining or complaining can wear any parent down. In the heat of the moment, we tend to blurt out words that only add fuel to the fire. It is easy for us to become trapped into the child's negative behavior by resorting to comments that threaten, "If you don't stop your whining right now, I'll. . . ." We might yell out an order, "Stop your crying this minute!" Or we name call, "You're a spoiled baby." But these destructive messages deal a devastating blow to the child's self-esteem. It is easy to get caught up in a competitive game of control, rich with frustration and with angry emotions that will get us nowhere.

We can eliminate frustration for both the parent and the child if we start by letting our children know that we understand their feelings, "I understand how much fun you are having playing outside." By approaching the problem in this fashion, we are letting them know that we understand their feelings, and we are helping them to identify their emotions.

"Do you remember that we have friends coming for dinner? We agreed that you will need to have your homework finished in order to join us this evening. I think you'll want to be a part of the activities tonight; if so, you'll need to do your homework. Why don't you take five minutes and finish what you're doing and then come in. I'll let you know when five minutes is up if you like."

When communicating with children, remember these steps. First, state your feelings: "I'm angry that you left your dog without water on this hot day." Next, state your expectation: "I expect you to fill his water dish every day." Finally, show how to make amends: "What your dog needs now is a bowl of fresh water." Help them come up with a solution to prevent further miscommunication. In addition, children need to learn that their actions have consequences and that their behavior impacts others. "What needs to be done in the future so that you'll remember to give your dog fresh water?" Listen carefully to the response and work to help them construct a solution to the problem. Because the child is vested in the resolution, he or she will be more likely to follow through in the future. A parent's parting words should always be positive. Praising your child's contribution and effort will have a more lasting impression than correcting the mistake.

Opening Positive Communication

Our role as parents is one of leader and guide for our children. Since guides know the trail, they are aware of the pitfalls. Positive leaders speak in positive language, "Watch your step," instead of

"Don't fall." When parents model positive leadership, the effect will overflow into the child-pet relationship.

The family pet offers a wonderful opportunity for children to learn how to communicate positively. Parents can initiate this process by using positive words with their children.

"You and your horse worked so hard to perfect that routine. I love the way you praised your horse with words of encouragement and a pat. I know that you wanted to practice more but were wise to recognize that your horse is tired. That was really thoughtful to respond to his need to rest."

Praise is a marvelous way to promote positive dialogue by helping children to feel good about themselves. Acknowledgement motivates positive behavior and builds self-esteem. There are numerous ways to implement positive reinforcement in everyday life.

Acknowledge what your child does right. It is important to describe the incident that was praiseworthy. Be specific. "I know you didn't want to go out in the rain to feed the chickens this morning, but you did without my reminding you. Good for you!"

Describe what you feel. "I felt so happy when I saw that you gave kitty clean food and water. I'm sure he feels happy, too." Even if we have to reprimand our child, we can still use a positive approach. Using language that describes your feelings will help to keep emotions separated from the discussion. "When you hit and yanked Spike during your training lesson today, it made me feel sad and disappointed. I'm sure that it made Spike sad, too."

> "A family is a unit composed not only of children, but of men, women, an occasional animal, and the common cold."
>
> -Ogden Nash

Sum up the child's praiseworthy behavior. "You hung your bridle and halter and put the brush and curry comb in their box. Now that's good organization!"

Another way for parents to promote positive dialogue with their child is to ask questions that require more than one-word answers. This opens the door to finding out what is really on their child's mind: "Tell me more about. . . ." or "I see that you had a hard day; exactly what didn't go well?"

When a young person sees differently from a parent, it takes a lot of courage to speak his mind. As parents, we tend to believe we are always right. Therefore, we have the tendency to argue with the youngster in an attempt to persuade. "Uh-huh, OK, but your mom and I...."

"I'm interested in what you think. Let's go in the other room where it's quiet so I can listen." Those are powerful statements because they convey to the young person that his or her opinion matters and that you value what the child has to say. It is important to acknowledge your child's point of view even if it conflicts with your own.

When we argue in an attempt to convince our children that we are right and they are wrong, we make them feel bad about their judgment, and the door of communication may close. It is more productive for parents to phrase their disagreement something like, "I don't agree with you. But you have the right to your own opinions. Let's take a few minutes and talk about this." Asking questions is the best way to find out what is really on the young person's mind. It can also help them draw conclusions as they hear aloud what they are saying.

When feelings are hard to say out loud, keeping a journal can be helpful for children to understand what might be troubling them. Writing engages a different part of the brain and may, therefore, unlock emotions that were previously inaccessible.

For teenagers, it is especially important to ask questions and stay away from statements: "Have you thought about what might happen if you . . .?" or perhaps just a simple comment such as "I'm sure you are aware of how your dad and I feel, but the choice is yours." Now the tough part: stand back and let it happen; allow the teen to make his or her decision. Unless the situation is one that would put the teen in harm's way, the parent needs to allow the young adult to proceed with his or her choice even if that choice is contrary to the parent's wishes.

If the choice fails, refrain from the tempting "I told you so." Instead, offer support for the teen's effort at independence by saying something such as "I'm sorry. I know how much you wanted this to happen."

Cathi Cohen specializes in child and family therapy. "Empathy," she says, "is the capacity to feel and think by observing verbal and nonverbal cues. It requires a person to:

1) Concentrate on the communication and the experience of another person.

2) Notice the behavior of the other person and understand what is being communicated through that behavior.

3) Be aware of the feelings of the other person without judging.

4) Respond appropriately."

When children tune us out, writing a note takes less out of us than opening our mouths and is oftentimes heard more clearly. And, children of all ages love receiving notes. Little ones are thrilled to receive a message from Mom or Dad. It encourages them to write or draw notes back to their parents. Teenagers view it as getting a letter from a friend. They are touched that their parents took the time to write to them.

Dear Crystal,
Please do something about your
boots in the hallway and coat
on the floor.
Thanks in advance----love, Mom

Dear Ben,
Your horse's stall needs cleaning.
Thanks ----love, Dad

Dear Nathan,
I haven't been out since this morning. Give me a break.
Your dog, Maggie

Alone at Home

Time alone doesn't have to be anxious; it can be happy and productive. The family pet can play a vital role in facilitating feelings of security. When the child opens the door, he or she knows there is a friend waiting inside, a friend to talk to and to play with.

Communication plays an important part as parents strive to provide a safe atmosphere for their children when they are home alone after school for short periods. It is helpful for parents to post safety rules as a reminder for their children.

Feeding and caring for the family pet before beginning home-work can be a great mental and physical break. Most all children hit the kitchen the minute they get in the door. Having snacks prepared ahead of time promotes not only better snack choices but also safety in the kitchen. Leave a note on the fridge, "If you're hungry, so is Buffy. Don't forget her snack too."

This is also a good time for cleaning a pet's housing and making sure it has fresh water. Parents can leave little notes posted around the house, like a treasure hunt, to help the child remember these responsibilities. The notes should be positive and reinforce good behavior.

Johnny,

Hope your day was great! When the house is quiet, it's a good time to do homework.

Love, Mom

Dear Betty,

I'm so proud of you and Buffy for remembering to finish your homework before you turned on your Gameboy.

Love, Mom

Dear Mike,

Remember that Buffy needs to be walked before you sit down to do your homework. You know how she hates to start thinking before she has played.

Love You, Mom

When a child involves the family pet in the task of doing homework, it will become more enjoyable and will help the youngster concentrate for longer periods of time. The more time a child interacts with the family pet, the less time he is likely to spend in front of the TV or playing video games.

Having the family pet at home with your child can be a great benefit. However, parents must remember that younger children should never be left unattended with an animal. This is for the safety for both the child and the family pet.

Parenting styles vary. There is no one right way to raise a child. But all involve effective communication between parent and child. Communicating with care and understanding is the key to developing strong and lasting relationships.

Helping our children to dis-cover who they are is sometimes a challenging task. But this job becomes enjoyable and rewarding when we join them as they explore, dream, and develop their unique talents. Throughout life, we have developed our own opinions and perceptions. Although we will share these insights with our children, we should not use them to confine our child's independence. Parents need to be sensitive that the journey they are sharing is also that of their child's. Sharing is a cooperative venture, a give and take between parent and child. Before we can take in what our child has to give, we must let go of some of our beliefs and views.

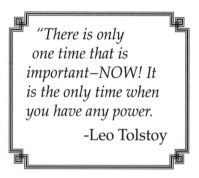

"There is only one time that is important—NOW! It is the only time when you have any power.

-Leo Tolstoy

One afternoon, a wise man invited his friend to tea. They talked of many things. No matter the subject, the visitor had something to say. He had so many opinions that the wise man finally gave up trying to participate in the conversation. Instead, he turned his attention to making tea.

As was custom, he poured his visitor's tea first, a full cup of tea, and then to his visitor's astonishment, he kept pouring. The visitor watched the overflow until he couldn't restrain himself. "It's overfull. No more will go in."

"Like this cup," replied the wise man, "you are so full of opinions my words will not go in."

AN OPEN HEART: PETS IN OUR LIFE

"Until he extends the circle of his compassion to all living things, man will not himself find peace."
                                                        -Albert Schweitzer.

By opening our homes and hearts to pets, we throw nature's window wide open and breathe deeply of her nourishment. Humans are predisposed to bond with other animals. Pets remain our connection to nature; they bring out and inspire the best in humanity. In order for our family pet to work its magic, we need to provide an enriching atmosphere for our animal friend. Part of this enrichment includes engaging our pet's inherent intelligence. The joy and value of the relationship that your family will have with your pet will be directly related to that animal's quality of life. Although quality of life is difficult to assess, it must be considered as important as clean water, fresh food, and a warm place to sleep. The affirmation of all life begins by teaching the positive treatment of pets to our children.

Animals offer much to a family. Pets are loyal and accept us as we are. They provide parents with teaching opportunities and children with playmates. They invite social interaction and are a stimulus for learning and creativity. They are a conduit for unconditional love and offer a good listening ear. Together pets and children form a secret world where a child can share thoughts and feelings they know will never be betrayed.

In our hurried and harried world, animals retain a natural pace. Pets behave in a more predictable fashion than people. Children thrive on routine. Taking care of a pet provides stability. This can be a comfort to children when they are trying to make sense of a world that is often confusing and frightening. Although as parents we may be preoccupied by our daily problems, the family pet will always be willing to give the time to a child, to play with or reassure him.

As a child I was raised by an assortment of nature's teachers, both four- and two-legged. Our milk cow refused to be a part of the herd, preferring instead the company of humans. She would often join us on an evening stroll or for moonlight ski-  *ing. We had a horse that enjoyed sledding. Imagine lying flat on a sled, careening down a slope and right behind you, a full-grown horse, galloping gleefully in your wake. We had a cat that wandered in magically from the woods one Christmas Eve and permanently planted herself in my sister's heart. And a small silkie chicken, Sarah, was most content when sitting perched like a squat falcon on an outstretched arm.*

There were other animals that graced our ranch, including some wonderful dogs, but these out of the ordinary characters are the ones that remain riveted in my mind and heart.

Summer evenings in Montana were an invitation for us to walk the mountain trail that began just outside our back door. We would breathe the last vestiges of the day's warm scent and watch night stars pop magically into the twilight sky. Up the path, single file we would proceed, my dad, my mother, myself, my sisters, our dogs (Blue and Just Dog), Smokey (the horse), Buttercup (the milk cow), and taking up the rear, Kitty. How funny we thought it was to be accompanied by this Noah's ark, and how privileged we felt to be deemed worthy.

In later years, after my academic training in animal behavior, I wondered what prompted them to join us. I still find it fascinating that they chose to trudge up a mountain trail with a host of humans rather than fill their bellies with tender blades of grass. The dogs I could understand. Following a pack leader is a part of their nature. But what about the horse and the cow? Was their participation merely a desire to be a part of a herd? What an odd clan to belong to. What about the cat? What was she doing with this strange assortment? Did these domesticated followers merely see us as leaders of an eclectic group, or did our laughter, affectionate touches, and genuine delight in their company encourage their participation? Did we give them something intangible and intrinsically satisfying, just as they did for us?

- Christine Hamer

According to Marty Becker, people enrich the lives of their pets much more than previously thought. Becker found in his veterinarian practice that animals recovered more quickly if their human family came to visit. It seems that our pets need our companionship as much as we need theirs.

There is no greater love than to recognize love between species and within other species quite distinct from our own. This is what I've learned as well in my life with animals, and this is what leads me deeper into a bond that, like the humpback's embrace, lifts me again and again to the surface.

- Brenda Peterson

People sometimes forget that our pets are not human animals but are infused with their own unique nature. For instance, a cat finds the moving of a leaf irresistible, responding to the innate desire to stalk and pounce. Our pets don't worry about the price of gas or tomorrow's meeting; the very moment they are living is all that matters. The world is one big game. For animals, play has a purpose. It gives them the opportunity to try out new behaviors and provides the chance to practice and refresh dormant skills. In other words, play is essential for an optimum life.

Our pet's engaging play helps to bring us in contact with nature's sense of humor. It allows us to laugh both with our pet and with ourselves. When we play with our animals, we remain in the here and now.

When I am focusing on [my dog] Sirloin, I am not think-ing about what I'm going to do when I get back, and he's not thinking about next year or how to realize his full Lab poten-tial. He's not even thinking, really. He's much too fascinated by the world right under his nose".

- Marty Becker.

When children are young, they wonder about the uniqueness of other living creatures, how some have fur and others have feath-ers. They marvel at how some can fly, some can run like the wind, yet others have scales and can swim under water. As a society, we've moved away from the heart of nature. Our children are lost in a world that is just a mouse click away and devoid of life. As parents,

we often hurry our child's journey and then shudder to realize how much has been lost. A child's unbridled fantasies and boundless imaginations are boxed tightly and labeled "Do Not Open." Gladys Blue, in *The Value of Pets in Children's Lives*, writes that humane treatment of both people and animals should be learned in the earliest years of life and that, in fact, this may be crucial. It is during childhood and adolescence that we instill the essence of humanity.

Angry adolescents often feel alienated in an adult world. They have been weaned on TV and video games. They have doubts about who they are and how they will fit in. But even the most jaded teenage mind can recapture childhood wonderment when the child relates to animals.

My friend Molly is a middle school teacher and has the difficult task of engaging cynical teenage boys. On the back of her classroom door is a poster of a kitten, "Hang in there Baby," that draws a response even from the "too cool to talk in class" kids. Echoes from the boxed dreams of childhood escape their baggy-jean clad bodies in soft sighs and coos of delight.

- Christine Hamer

Many homes already own pets but are not allowing them to become full family members. Confining a bird or small mammal solely to its cage or a dog to a kennel not only restricts the animal's natural movement but robs the family of the enjoyment of the pet's true and unfettered nature. Allowing a pet into the family will give intangible qualities to both ourselves and our children if we allow them to become an integral part of our lives.

When we adopt other species and love them as our own, this is the best of all possible worlds. This is embracing more than our own kind, and assuring that more than we alone will survive. For if humans survive without the company of other animals, then we will be more alone than any of our ancestors could ever have imagined. To one day find ourselves on this ocean planet alone with only our own kind would be the beginning of the end of our species."

- Brenda Peterson

I have one of the fattest ducks in the world. I bought him, his brother, and his sister about three years ago; their names were Duck, Duke, and Ducky. Those ducks would follow me anywhere. Every night, after I let them loose into the pond, they would come up to get a bite to eat. We bonded to a point you would think duck and boy couldn't bond.

My mom trains hunting dogs for a living. At this time we had a dog named Tigger. My mom had been training him for a hunting dog. It seemed like no threat to me at the time.

One day I went down to feed my ducks. My mom had let Tigger out for a run. I heard commotion down by the pond. I saw Tigger grab Duke by the body. I dumped the food out of the food dish and ran at him screaming. My other ducks had dashed down to the pond. Tigger who still squeezed my duck tight in his mouth was now running the other way. I took my food dish and threw it at him. It hit him hard on the head, giving me time to run up and seize him by the fur. I shoved my hand into his mouth and pried it open. My duck came rolling out onto the grass. My mom, hearing me scream, came down and grabbed Tigger. Duke laid there on the ground, his mouth slightly open and his eyes opening and closing. I slowly moved my hand across his back, ruffling soft feathers. I saw two teeth marks in his body. Duke stooped his head down. His wings were out like he was trying to pull himself up. I knew in my heart that he was not going to make it, yet I stayed there.

"What do you want to do honey?" my mom asked in a sweet yet sad voice.

"Just give me a last minute with him," I said through tears. She left with Tigger and went up to the barn to put him away. Duke lay still, almost dead. I reached down and felt his soft feathers and his heart pounding. He looked at me with his eyes,

and I looked straight back. It was a look I'll never forget. Then he stopped breathing and closed his eyes.

What I learned from Duke is that a friendship is a wonderful gift, and I am glad for every moment I had with him. Any special gift like that should be cherished forever. Now, my last duck always comes up to get food, and I am ready to feed him.

- Nathan Hamer, age 11

LOVE UNCONDITIONAL

"I have never felt pitied by an animal or judged."
                                                    - Brenda Peterson

"Do you remember, when Buffy chewed up your football, how angry you felt? But you love her even though she chewed up your football?"
"Yes."
"Just like you love Buffy, I will always love you."

The greatest gift parents can give their child is unconditional love. But learning this is not easy. We can't pick it up, like a cup of milk, and say to our child, "This is unconditional love; it will always be here," and then place it on display for them to remember. Instead, we need to demonstrate it everyday with our words and by our actions.

This is especially true during times we feel disappointed or frustrated with our child's behavior. We can let the child know that, although we may not approve of his behavior, we still love him. No matter what he does, our love is not conditional on his behavior.

One of our challenges as parents is to help our children distinguish between them, as people, and their actions. Sometimes entangled in their problems, children may think, "I really screwed up this time. Mom and Dad won't love me anymore." And, during an upset, we tend to focus on the problem. This is the point where we need to be careful with the words we choose to talk with our children. Senseless words can make them believe that they are a failure. They may fear they're no longer loved by the two most important people in their life, their parents.

As parents we tend to forget that our children's self-image is fragile. They need to feel their importance within our hearts is secure. We must guard against the impression that we measure our love according to our child's behavior. When a child misbehaves, he or she needs to know we don't love the child any less. When we model unconditional love, we separate the child's misbehavior from the unique and special child that we love.

> Tell them that it takes time to do something well. It is also important to point out that the task is not who they are.

"Yes, I'm angry with you. You made a choice to go home with Billie without talking with me first. When you didn't come home from school on time, I started to worry. It's not that I don't trust you, but I need to know that you're safe. I'd like you to think about this. Later we'll talk about how to prevent this from happening again. You know I still love you. Come here and let me give you a hug."

My husband and I watched the positive changes in our parenting as we witnessed the power of unconditional love from our pets. At times when our girls were disruptive, my husband and I were quick to give a harsh correction. We noticed how easily our pets could handle any emotional reaction from the girls. If we had taken a few minutes, we would have realized that our love for our daughters was more important than the minor

behavior problem at hand. Our pets reminded us uncondi-
tional love is a powerful gift.

- Margaret Hevel

The nonjudgmental companionship pets provide can restore balance in the whole family. Pets offer a different type of compassion than humans. A 1993 Harvard Health Letter stated that companion animals offer unconditional affection and they display more consistent behavior than human companions. Pets accept their humans without judging or criticizing.

At school, children sometimes experience days of frustration and hurt when classmates tease or ignore them. Spending time with a family pet can release the child's volatile emotions and help to restore his or her sense of well being.

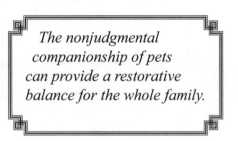

The nonjudgmental companionship of pets can provide a restorative balance for the whole family.

My daughter Tolene was learning how to ride again. When her father and I had divorced, we were forced to sell our horses. Tolene was only seven, but the loss of her friends hit her hard. Tolene became very quiet and bashful, uncertain of anything in life after loosing both a parent and her four-legged friends.

Our first purchase was a mistake. We bought a horse too spirited for a bruised child, trying to rebuild her battered soul. So we continued looking…newspapers, auctions, talking with friends.

Nothing stood out or felt right until we met some people at an auction. They told us about their aging horse that was "well-trained and loved people." They were looking for a younger horse that would be able to withstand the vigorous riding of a more advanced horseperson. In order to do this, they needed to sell the mare.

My daughter listened as they described the mare. I wasn't keen on looking at an aged horse that might develop health problems or worse…break my daughter's fragile heart. I was ready to decline politely when my daughter caught my eye. I could tell right away that she wanted, needed, to see this mare. Against my better judgment, I agreed.

What a shock! If it hadn't been for the mud, her ribs would have stuck out even further. Her foal of nine months had chewed the mare's tail and "nursed" away her nourishment. I almost turned around right then and there and walked away. But something held me. I think it was the look in my daughter's eyes. She was riveted to the horse. Quietly, she spoke to me, "Mom, we need to take her home."

I was starting to talk Tolene out of the idea when the man asked Tolene if she wanted to ride the mare. Up to this point, all I had seen was a scraggly, dirty old mare and a truckload of potential vet bills. But when my daughter settled herself into the saddle and turned to trot the mare around the pasture, I saw something I didn't quite believe. I thought I saw that mare smile.

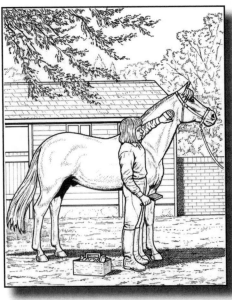

Like something out of the movies, Kelly's and Tolene's spirits connected. Tolene hadn't looked that good in the saddle or smiled that widely in a long time. At that point, I would have paid any price for that

mare. The man said if we could give Kelly a good home, he would make us a deal.

We trimmed her feet and hoped her tail would grow back. Tolene nearly brushed the hide off Kelly. Each stroke was one of love. It wasn't long before that mare began to shine. They developed their own language. Their love grew in leaps and bounds. When Kelly came into Tolene's life, my daughter had just turned eleven. She learned that with love and effort, you could always improve. Kelly taught her compassion and responsibility.

Sometimes when Kelly was resting in her stall, Tolene would lie against her, caressing Kelly. Tolene loved to watch Kelly raise her head in the air and curl her lips after drinking a Pepsi with her. Then Kelly would nudge my daughter in the shoulder for more.

One morning when I went out to feed, I knew something wasn't right. I called my daughter, and we loaded Kelly into the trailer and took her to the vet. The day we dreaded had arrived. Without guarantee that she would make it through surgery, we chose not to put Kelly through any unnecessary pain. With our hearts breaking, we took her home.

We prepared a final resting place for Kelly. As we waited for the vet, it started to rain. We protected her from the rain as best we could. The vet gave Kelly the relief she had earned and deserved. As Kelly took her last breath, the rain stopped and a rainbow arched the sky. It was the most beautiful I had ever seen. My daughter and I held each other as Kelly followed the path to heaven.

- Bonnie Borkhuis

Our children make choices daily: what to say, what to wear, what to do, and which friends to follow. They are buffeted by many influences that can shake the core values we have worked so hard to instill. As parents, we can fortify our children with the foundation of unconditional love. Our family pet can become our partner, helping us to give our children a love as constant as the rising and setting of the sun and moon. This base will keep them strong through the deluge of false promises. Unconditional love forms a force field strong enough to repel the stabs at their self-esteem.

Unconditional love forms a safety net for our children to experiment. They will feel safe to try different things and to make mistakes because they know we will always be there. Like artists on the flying trapeze, they can stretch for greater heights and reach for longer flights.

TRUST AND FAITH

*"You can tell about a people of a country by the
way they treat their animals."*
-Mahatma Gandhi

Trust is a two-way street. It must be given before it can be received. In Deepak Chopra's book *Seven Spiritual Laws for Parents*, he explains, "If you want to get something, give it." We must earn trust and respect through our words and by our deeds in any relationship. This is especially evident in our relationships with our children and the family pets. To gain their complete trust, parents must give from the heart. Adults have learned to guard carefully their hearts from what they perceive as a hurtful world. But when we protect ourselves from hurt, we become inaccessible. We prove ourselves trustworthy when our children can see our vulnerability. In this way our children learn that their tender feelings are also safe in the family.

Lessons in loyalty and trust are all around us. They can be seen in the trusting offer of a child who places a hand within ours or in the level gaze of faith that shines from the eyes of the family pet.

I remember Ginger through a child's eyes. Half-Tennessee walker, she strode with that rocking horse gait of her heritage.

She was the center of our childhood Wild West fantasies. On Ginger, my sister and I would ride the range with Roy Rogers, mending the fences and branding cattle. She would wait patiently by our afternoon campfires made from brown paper bags colored yellow orange, while we sipped lemonade from Bonanza tin cups.

As I grew older, Ginger nourished my teenage fantasies of freedom, taking me on winged flights across fields, crisscrossed with irrigation ditches that we cleared at break-neck speeds. Other times, we walked in quiet contemplation, absorbing nature.

She was a horse with a gentle nature, especially with children. I'll never forget when my younger sister, only two, wandered unattended into Ginger's pasture. The horse was lying down, relaxing, when the toddler crawled onto her back. In general, horses stand when approached by humans; perhaps Ginger saw the babe as no threat. She remained still while my sister kicked at her sides and hollered for her to "get a-going." Somehow the mare knew. Perhaps deep within her heart beat the instinct of motherhood. She remained frozen, lest a shift in her weight would cause the child to tumble from her back.

Now as a mother, I can appreciate what my mother must have felt when she found my missing sister and the potential for danger. It must have taken every ounce of courage not to panic. Her calmness was essential, as the horse would take my mother's demeanor as a cue for her own behavior. She approached Ginger, one mother to another and the mare seemed to understand. Ginger suppressed the flight-urge inherent in a prey animal, the desire to jump to her feet, ready for escape. She allowed herself to be vulnerable so my mother could retrieve the child from her back. The instant that the child was free, Ginger stood, shook with a teeth-jarring tremor, then walked away.

- Christine Hamer

Our world today is filled with more opportunities for mistrust than with chances to forge a loving and interactive relationship. This basic lack of trust and faith in our fellow human beings is an issue that should be on the political table yet seems to be a subject that everyone skirts. It is difficult to trust when it seems as though the world is filled with lies. Truth from politicians is colored by their upcoming election, and it feels as though every person involved in resolving conflicts has an ulterior motive. The ability to search continually for positive aspects in an apprehensive world is a gift to bestow upon our children.

The underlying hope that we can give our children in these uncertain times comes from the lessons learned from animals, trust in life. Allowing ourselves to be vulnerable and trusting our heart to another makes us trustworthy. Our pets will trust us unless that trust is breached. They trust that we will keep them from harm's way. The animals that behave the most heroically have the most faith in humanity. Witnessing these lessons of pure faith and trust is a gift that we, as parents, can point out to our children.

Snow came early our first Montana winter. We skied through the woods, down the hill, and along our meadow. We harvested Christmas trees on the hillside. Our daughters gathered the pine boughs, stacked them in the pickup, and sold them in town. At home, they rushed to drop coins into their savings banks. A week before Christmas, they made secret trips into stores, hunting for family gifts. Scotch tape fastened festive wrapping paper. Packages were hidden under beds, beneath clothing in dresser drawers, and deep in closet corners.

Christmas Eve, Joanne called from the backdoor, "Daddy, hurry!"

"What's the matter, Jo?"

"A kitty is stuck in our tree. I called 'Kitty, kitty.' But she won't come down."

Outside, we heard plaintive meowing from pine branches twenty feet above the ground.

"Daddy, we need a ladder."

"Our ladder isn't long enough, pumpkin."

"Give her a little time," I said. "We'll check on her after dinner."

We did. She remained out of reach.

Snow fell while the girls hung their stockings from the mantle. We snuggled on the couch while I read Christmas stories. When I finished the last one, Joanne patted my cheek.

"One more try?"

Snow boots were pulled on and coats zipped. The kitten was perched on a branch half way down the pine tree. Joanne called, "Kitty, kitty." The kitten dropped into her waiting arms. Joanne nestled her cheek against the dark gray fur. "Wait until the others see."

A pillowcase was stuffed with rags. Like a feline princess from a fairytale, gray kitty snuggled into her bed. Four soft voices whispered, "Goodnight, kitty."

"Do you think the kitty will like our home?" Joanne asked.

"Honey . . . she may not be able to live with us."

"But, Mommy, she's God's Christmas present to me. I can't return her."

"Maybe she belongs to another little girl and got lost in the snowstorm."

"No. I know she'll live with us. Don't worry . . . she's not lost."

"We have to make sure. Tomorrow we'll put an ad in the paper. "I kissed her forehead and cheeks. "If no one calls after a week . . . gray kitty has a home with us."

Joanne's arms wrapped around my neck, "I love you Mommy."

"I love you too."

Whenever the phone rang that week, Joanne squeezed her eyes shut and crossed her fingers. Sunday night finally came and so did her sigh of relief. An official naming ceremony never took place. Waving her crooked tail and giving a soft meow, she came to the call of . . . Gray Kitty.

That winter, Gray Kitty joined us skiing down the wooded hillsides. She ran between our skis. When she stopped to chew snowballs in her paws, Joanne scooped her up, unzipped her jacket and tucked her inside for the rest of the run.

In the spring, Gray Kitty's equestrian lessons began. She rode inside Joanne's backpack, only her head poked out. On later horseback rides, Gray Kitty was draped over the saddle in front of Joanne while they rode into imaginary adventures along our meadow and forest trails.

Joanne became her father's star pupil in the art of milking our Guernsey cow. Gray Kitty never missed a squirt of warm milk while Joanne filled the milk pail topped with a head of foam.

One summer evening at milking time, Grey Kitty failed to appear. A pitiful "meow" answered our call. We found her curled up in the bushes back of the chicken coop. Part of her jaw was missing. Gently, I lifted her and placed her in Joanne's arms. Gray Kitty never moved on the long drive to town nor did she struggle while Joanne held her during the doctor's examination.

"Look's like someone shot your cat," said the vet. "She has a fifty-fifty chance." At home, we fed her soft nourishing meals, irrigated the wound, and administered antibiotics. We watched and waited. Gray Kitty rested and healed. Later that summer, she returned to horseback riding with Joanne.

The years slipped by to the fall when Joanne packed her clothes for college. She stroked the cat's stomach. "See you at Thanksgiving." Gray Kitty disappeared the day after Joanne left.

Snow dusted our pine trees the day Joanne came home in November. Late afternoon, Joanne told her father, "I'll milk Buttercup tonight." Gray Kitty walked in with Buttercup at milking time and left when Joanne returned to college after the holiday.

This routine connection between Joanne and her feline partner continued until the following September when Joanne filled boxes for college. While patting Gray Kitty, she told her childhood friend, "Now don't go on any adventures without me."

Maybe Gray Kitty sensed the days of Joanne playing dress-up, swinging her on the hammock, and taking her skiing or horseback riding in her backpack were over. Her Joanne was grown up, ready to venture forth on her own. Gray Kitty left that next day and never came home again.

In memories, the nurturing spirit from a feline angel, Gray Kitty, continues to shine in this woman's childhood heart.

- Margaret Hevel

WILL ANY PET DO?

Before you buy any pet, the first family project is to research the biology, characteristics, and physical requirements of the animal you are considering. Some of the questions you should answer are:

1) How long does this pet live?

2) How large does this pet grow?

3) How much space does this animal need to have an optimal life?

4) What kind of grooming and vet care does the pet require?

5) What kind of exercise does this animal need and how often? Some pets require training time in addition to regular care.

6) What does this animal eat and how much?

7) What is the daily care regimen for this kind of pet, and does our family realistically have the time?

8) Are there any allergies or other sensitivities among family members that might conflict with having this type of pet? Parrots can be quite noisy for sound sensitive people. Rodents may be odoriferous for those more sensitive to smells.

At a minimum, the following must be provided for a pet to have quality life: safe housing, nutritious food and clean water, routine and emergency medical care, exercise, mental stimulation, attention and understanding, behavioral limits–generally set out through training, and love and respect.

Take a realistic look at family lifestyle. Will your family have the time to provide adequately for the pet you are considering? If members are running from dance recitals to soccer practice, who will be responsible for your pet's training and exercise? These are requirements as important as clean water and nourishing food. This is not to say that a busy family cannot own a pet. But there must be a commitment among all family members to allocate the time needed for the new pet.

The lifespan of an animal should be a major consideration for parents. Although children will become more responsible and able to care more fully for their animals as they grow older, they will eventually leave home. Some animals are quite long-lived, and although none of us can predict the future, whatever plans the family makes should include the welfare of the pet.

If your family moves frequently, be aware that some locations may not allow larger pets such as cats and dogs. Consider a smaller, more transportable pet such as fish, or a gerbil may be a better choice. Sometimes the best decision might be to choose not to have a pet. It is never easy to say "no" to a child, especially when there is a part of us that desires to have a pet in our lives as well. However consider the fact that it will be much more difficult for all involved if faced with the trauma of needing to re-home a beloved family member at a future date.

Even if the family decides that getting a pet at this time isn't the best option, children can still enjoy sharing their lives with an animal. Consider allowing the children to pet-sit a friend's pet or to bring home the classroom pet from school. (Also, see the next chapter, "Nature in the Lives of Children.")

One important consideration is matching your choice of pet to the maturation level of your child. For instance, small children or those with behavioral problems are not the best matches for a small or delicate pet. A sturdier animal will also fare better for those children with developing motor skills.

The responsibility level of the child and the needs of the pet should complement each other. Responsibility requires keeping an agreement, namely the one to care for the pet. Sometimes parents equate the size of the pet with the size of the responsibility. Although the tasks may be smaller with pint-sized pets, the commitment is the same. There is no magic age at which a child is capable of understanding the importance of daily care of an animal. This will depend on the individual maturity of each child. Therefore, parents must assess their family in general and the older children in particular and gauge the readiness to adopt a pet. (See the section, "Responsibility," in the earlier chapter, "The Role of a Pet in the Changing Child.")

Pet stores tend to be the first resource most people consider when looking for small pets. These include small rodents such as hamsters, gerbils and mice, rabbits, fish, and small birds such as canaries and budgies. Some of the larger stores will carry such animals as hedgehogs, prairie dogs, ferrets, monkeys, and reptiles (turtles, snakes and iguanas). Although these may be acceptable places to obtain these types of pets, not all animals available in pet stores are good choices for children.

Reptiles can transmit the salmonella bacteria in their feces. Because these animals live in a confined space when in captivity, the bacteria tend to be prevalent on their skin. Salmonella is transmitted by direct contact, such as touching or handling the animals. If you choose to have a reptile or amphibian as a pet, teach the children to follow strict procedures for hand-washing and disinfections. You will also need to pay special attention to the cleanliness of the cage and quality of the animal's food and water–the cleaner the environment, the fewer bacteria and other diseases. Because these pets tend not to be very interactive, they make better pets for older children who maybe interested in them as a study of nature and adaptation.

Some pet stores also carry puppies and kittens. Whereas fish can be kept in a minimally enriched environment with few psychological side effects, this is not true for cats and dogs. Living developmental years in confinement with minimal human contact can have long-lasting behavioral repercussions. Often puppies sold in pet stores originated from a puppy mill, casting doubt regarding the puppy's heritage and health.

For more information on selecting a dog, personalities of different breeds, and questions to ask a breeder, see the reference section or visit the Website, www.dogsensecentral.com.

There are specialty clubs for a wide variety of birds and animals. These clubs would be great for starting your search for the best place to adopt the companion animal of your choice, whether it's fur, fin, or feather. Animal shelters become repositories for all sorts of unwanted pets. Perhaps your perfect companion is waiting for your family at your local Humane Society. By adopting a pet from one of these sources, you are not only gaining a family friend;

you are also giving a much needed home to an animal waiting to be loved.

Once your family has decided on what type of pet you are looking for–reptile, bird, fish, or mammal–consult specific books to help you hone in on the best breed. Cats, rabbits, gerbils, hamsters, dogs, and horses, all of which are the most common warm and fuzzy pets, have subsets within the larger groups. Just as cats act differently from dogs, breeds within each group have specific personalities, exercise requirements, and grooming and feeding needs. Dogs are especially assorted in the range of size, shape, personality, and maintenance requirements.

In addition to books, consult a veterinarian, local trainer, animal shelter, and breeder. Ask friends and neighbors about their experiences in pet ownership, in general, and if possible, find someone who has owned the breed you are researching to ask more specific questions. These people will let you know about the problems and the joys they have experienced with the pet you are considering.

Some animals should never be considered for pets. Wild animals, even when hand-raised from babies, are not candidates. People are under the misconception that when acquired at a young age, wild animals can be domesticated. However, they can carry disease and parasites that can be transmitted to family members. Most important, the wild characteristics of the animal's nature emerge as the animal approaches adolescence. Biological drives and instincts that are normal for an animal to express in its natural environment can be dangerous when in the close company of humans.

Wild animals are best enjoyed in their native environment. Children should be taught to respect wild animals and to allow them to live in the world they were meant to inhabit. Children should never touch, feed, or take home a wild animal.

Although domesticated animals are generally safe, any animal can become dangerous if forced into self-defense. Some animals that might be appropriate as pets may not be tolerant of children if they haven't been socialized around them from an early age. When your pet first comes home, take it to a veterinarian to make sure that it is healthy. We also recommend consulting a trainer or behavioral specialist before finalizing your purchase or adoption, especially when considering a cat or dog because of the potential for injury from bites. Animals are substantial investments of both money and time. The quality of the family's interaction with its new pet will depend on a good match of personalities.

Judicious parents can avoid many pet-child accidents. According to Brian Kilcommons, a dog behaviorist and author, the number-one cause of dog bites to children is from the lack of parental supervision. He says, "Leaving a dog alone with a child is like leaving two toddlers in the same room with a pair of scissors."

Children must be taught proper behavior around their new pet, and the pet needs to be taught how to respond appropriately to children. Some pets learn to bite and scratch because children pull their ears or tails, squeeze them, drop them, fall on them, or startle them by picking them up too fast.

Before interacting with your pet, learn to "read" how your pet displays discomfort, fear, anger, and joy. (See the earlier chapter, "Pets Teach *Tolerance.*") Understand the signs that indicate your pet is becoming uncomfortable or frightened. You can help your pet by altering your behavior before it is forced to defend himself. If your pet is severely uncomfortable around your family, even after you have taken all of the steps to help it feel at home, please seek the assistance of a behavior specialist.

People enjoy a place of solitude, a quiet space. Just like their humans, animals also need a place to get away from the commotion of active family life. Children should learn to be respectful of their animal's needs. One of the best ways to instill this is to teach mutual acceptance, love, and respect. Treat the animal with kindness, and you should receive the same. Don't disturb animals while they are sleeping or eating. Give them a spot where they can retreat for peace and quiet.

Be aware of your pet's tolerance level for activity and stressful situations. If your pet is generally more solitary, and the family is planning a party, help your pet to handle the unusual activity by placing it in a quiet place well ahead of the festivities. It is unfair to force the pet to participate.

Buying a New Pet

This section is not designed to be a complete care guide, rather a general overview of considerations of the most common animals selected as pets.

We hesitate to write time requirements needed for the care of each pet since some people may misunderstand. The times are estimates for the care and feeding, in other words, the minimum time needed to keep the animal in good health. Additional time is needed to develop an optimal relationship. Even quiet moments spent simply watching the animal will leave you with a deeper appreciation for nature and a greater understanding of the diversity of life. The rewards your family will gain from investing time with your pet are priceless.

Easy Starter Pets

Fish

Fish are often a good first pet. They are low maintenance and teach children the basics of pet ownership and responsibility. There are more fish kept in American homes than any other type of pet, according to Mary Jane Checchi in *Are You the Right Pet for Me?* They don't have any of the problems associated with larger pets such as drooling, shedding, or associated allergies. They won't keep you up all night or destroy the house, and they exercise and entertain themselves.

> I really Love my fish. They are quiet. If they died I would not get more. They are special to me because they are part of our family. They make happy because I would be lonely if I did not have them

-Kenzie Potter, Grade 1

Most children like having a pet in their bedroom, and fish are ideal for this. The aquarium light can even double as a nightlight, offering a watery defense against closet monsters. This is also a great pet for people with fur-related allergies.

Children should be taught that fish "breathe" through their gills to obtain oxygen from their watery environment; therefore, they cannot be removed from the tank. Objects cannot be dropped into the tank because it is detrimental to the fish's health. Clean fresh water kept at the right temperature, balance of light and dark, and the proper diets are imperative for healthy, happy fish. Most diseases and health problems that fish experience are due to an imbalance in their aquatic environment.

Although fish can't be handled, children can still become intimately familiar with the differences in fish personalities. Encourage them to name the fish and watch for distinguishing characteristics. Feeding time is generally highly active and therefore a good time for fish watching. Be careful not to overfeed; fish require very little food.

Fish can be highly entertaining as children set up elaborate underwater villages for their gilled friends to swim around and through. Fish can be kept inside in salt water (a more costly and complex system), in fresh water, or outside (for some goldfish and koi). Some fish are of the "live bearer" group and will produce young, which can turn into a fun hobby.

Fish retain primitive characteristics and can become aggressive, attack, harass, and kill other fish. For sensitive children, this can be disconcerting. However, this will also provide an opportunity to talk about the basics of nature and such issues as birth and death. Some species are more gregarious than others. Check for compatibility before you bring home a new fish and add it to your aquarium.

Start up cost: From $20 for a nice, small aquarium up to $500 for a fancy salt water system.

Monthly maintenance costs: Expenses can range from $1 for a goldfish where you just change the water and sprinkle food to $50 for more elaborate systems.

Vet care: $0.

Daily time commitment: 10-15 minutes.

Hermit crabs

This is another low maintenance pet that can be kept in the child's room. In general, the hermit crab habitat is easier upkeep than an aquarium full of fish. These interesting creatures are scavengers so they can live on your table scraps. They will need larger shells to "re-home" as they grow, and watching them take on a new shell is part of the fun. Hermit crabs can teach a child rudimentary handling skills. The crabs should be handled by their shells to avoid having little fingers pinched. These interesting animals can open a variety of topics about nature and ecosystems, food-chains, habitats, and niche environments, to name a few.

I used to have hermit crabs but they died. I enjoyed them when they changed thier shells. and I felt good.

-Sameem Novooz Grade 1

Crabs can be quite entertaining. According to Mary Jane Checchi, six-year-old Reilly would spend hours constructing mazes out of blocks for his pets and then enjoy watching them navigate each maze.

Like fish, crabs need to have their enclosure cleaned regularly. Like all animals, the quality of their life and health will be determined by the cleanliness of their home and the quality of food they receive.

Hello, I am Martin Stewart and I would like to tell about my pet hermit crabs. First things first, Hermit crabs come from the Caribbean. Most are smaller than a normal crab and they carry a shell to hide in. My first hermit crab came from North Carolina.

My family was there for a vacation and my mom always gives me $20.00 to spend. I went to a special store and bought, 1 cage (wire) 1 crab, and a sponge all for $17.84. The next year I only bought one crab for I had everything else the crab would need.

My crabs seem to be able to talk. Sometimes, if I hurry by their cage they look at me as if to say, "Dude, get a life and relax." They have also taught me to be careful. Crabs are fragile and will break easily. I recommend them as pets for they have long lives, are inexpensive, and easy to care for. Every day they will make you smile.

-Martin Stewart, Grade 4

Start up cost: $10.

Monthly maintenance costs: $2. Although crabs are scavengers, in addition to food remnants, they need a vitamin supplement to help with their exoskeleton growth.

Vet care: $0.

Daily time commitment: 3-15 minutes, depending on how much time you spend watching them.

Gerbils, hamsters, mice, and rats:

These low maintenance critters are the least expensive of the "warm and fuzzy" group and also make great first pets. Unlike fish or crabs, these first-step pets introduce not only the concepts of pet ownership and responsibility but also the concept of gentle handling as well. Although pet stores are the most common places to obtain members of this group, don't rule out your local animal shelter. Sometimes families will purchase rodents without researching their habits. When the rodent's lifestyle clashes with the people, the pet is left with the local shelter in the hopes that the staff can find the animal a new home. After the release of a popular movie, such as "Stewart Little, " the story about a mouse with human characteristics, children with the hopes of having their very own Stewart purchased scores of the little white mice. Unfortunately these mice acted like, well, mice.

Although mice are generally hardy enough to be housed indoors or out (check with specific species information; not all will tolerate temperature fluctuations so this may not be an option in your area), they cannot tolerate rough handling. Small children will need to be watched closely so they don't injure the delicate creatures. Like most animals, they are not opposed to doling out a nip if they are handled too roughly. But if they are held gently and frequently from the time they are young, rodents can become quite affectionate. Rodents must gnaw to file their continuously growing incisors. Overgrown teeth cause health problems. Providing your pet with natural items to chew such as nuts, firm vegetables, or wood will remedy this issue.

Rodents prefer to have a companion close to their own size and species, but it might be best to get two of the same sex, unless you have plans to breed. Females coexist well, and their urine is less odiferous than the musky scent of males. The bedding should be changed regularly to keep the housing smelling sweet no matter what the sex of the inhabitant.

Although some of the members of this group can be housed together, be careful when planning cohabitation. Natural territorial tendencies between members of the same species and aggressive displays between different species (mice and rats, for instance) suggest that it is better to keep only families in a single enclosure.

In the wild, these animals have a larger home range than the confines of your cage, so, the larger the habitat, the better. Because your pet cannot leave this environment, it is very important that you make it as clean and mentally stimulating as possible. The happier your pet, the more interactive it will be with the family. A bored pet is more apt to develop health problems as well. Along these same lines,  the positioning of your pet's cage in your home will contribute to the animal's willingness to interact with members of the family. By setting your pet's home in a high traffic zone, you will not only remind yourself to say "hi" to your rodent friends, but you also provide a live "TV" for your furry friend.

One downside to these creatures is their nocturnal habits (oil that exercise wheel or you and the children will be up all night) and their relatively short life spans, generally about two to three years. They are more complex in their behavior and may also provide opportunity to talk about empathy, compassion, trust, and responsibility. Members of this group will also most likely provide you with role models for issues such as reproduction, birth, and death and help lead your child through the grieving process.

Set-up costs: $30 up to $200 for a fancy large playhouse. Animal cost varies from about $2 to $10, depending on the variety of rodent you choose.

Monthly maintenance costs: $7. Because there is so much variation between the different members of the rodent family as well as differences within the each variety, do the proper research to understand how to care for the pet you have selected.

Vet care costs: Although there is not routine veterinarian care for rodents, it may be difficult to locate a vet for their emergency care. I advise doing research to locate one in your area before you bring your pet home. If your animal does become sick, it is important to seek medical attention immediately as sick or injured rodents often die just a day or two after the onset of symptoms.

Realize that although this pet is inexpensive, it is a valued pet and friend of your child and are therefore not expendable. Ignoring a sick pet is the equivalent of ignoring the child's feelings. By treating the lowliest of animals as important, you display not only your value for life but for your child's fragile feelings as well.

Daily time commitment: 30 minutes.

Pets That Need More Care

Rabbits and guinea pigs

These animals offer a "baby-step" up from the rodents in terms of responsibility and care. Since they are slightly larger than the earlier mentioned rodent group, their accommodations must be larger, and their exercise and maintenance requirements are more demanding. Rabbits especially thrive with some outdoor time to nibble on green grass and soak up sunshine. Rabbits and guinea pigs can be housed indoors or outdoors but should have large warm quarters. They will need fresh food, a varied diet, and clean water daily. Cleaning their cage will place a greater demand on your time than that of the smaller rodents. Like rodents, rabbits need something to chew on to maintain dental health and prevent their teeth from growing too long. They also require a mineral block to keep them healthy.

Rabbits are social, naturally living in colonies; however, they need to be habituated to human handling. They are susceptible to stress related illness and should be handled quietly and frequently to help them overcome their natural prey instinct of fear. They like to dig and burrow, using tunnels for sleeping and to  raise their young. Because of their social habits, rabbits should not be housed alone as they can become ill or destructive. Companionship can also be in the form of different but compatible species, such as guinea pigs.

Rabbits can be taught to use a litter box and therefore can be given freedom to roam the house and become a more integral member of the family. Be careful however; rabbits do not discriminate between poisonous and non-noxious plants and will eat any houseplant within their reach. They can be quite ingenious when it comes to reaching a tasty morsel. I had a pet rabbit that was very clever about climbing her way up the backs of chairs in order to reach an otherwise inaccessible wandering Jew plant. She trimmed their lengthy strands down to dirt in no time flat.

Set up cost: In pet stores, you can get a $90 starter kit. This has minimal space for your pet, so we recommend creating an additional exercise area. A larger nice hutch costs around $250.

Monthly maintenance cost: $13-$15,

Vet care costs: Rabbits make better house companions when they are altered. This prevents them from spraying and exhibiting other habits most people find obnoxious. They are also more easily trained, calmer, and less aggressive. Neutering costs will vary with each location so it is best to check with your local veterinary clinic.

Rabbits have a delicate constitution and should get immediate vet attention should they show signs of illness. Like other "small furries, " they tend to decline quickly after the first signs of illness.

Daily time commitment: 30-45 minutes

Budgies, canaries, and finches

These small members of the avian family are a constant source of singing and chatter. This can be cheerful for some people and quite annoying to others. Canaries and finches are in the songbird family. Finches are social with their own kind, and enjoy sharing a large flight with others of their kind. Canaries tend to be more solitary, and males can fight if caged together. As a consequence, they do fine alone in a nice big cage. Neither of these types of  birds are particularly interactive with people, though they seem to enjoy human activity in their area. Budgies (a.k.a. budgerigars or "parakeets") are in the parrot family and are highly social and interactive. They thrive with the attention of a family but require patience to establish a trusting relationship. Budgies have loads of personality, and children love their sociable nature, flying to their shoulder and "helping" with their homework. Young children should be supervised around the small creatures since their fragile bones can be easily broken by over-amorous squeezes.

Because they are intelligent, budgies need time outside the confines of their cage daily. During their free-flight time, be aware of doors, windows, and other escape routes and potential hazards such as other family pets like dogs and cats. They need fresh food and water daily and their cages should be cleaned on a regular basis; the frequency will depend on how much time they spend within its confines. Birds require their toenails trimmed as a part of regular maintenance.

The bird's cage should be in a family area to enhance socialization but also one that can be darkened at night. Birds like height, so place the cage on a table, not on the floor. Another option is to buy a sturdy stand from which the cage can be hung. Also guard against temperature extremes. Like all pets, a good healthy well-balanced diet will keep your bird healthy and active well into old age. The proper diet depends on the species – but no species of bird thrives on an all seed diet, as vegetables and greens are important for health. They also enjoy regular baths or showers to keep their feathers clean.

If they are handled gently and consistently from the time they are young, budgies can be quite friendly, affectionate and curious. We have found that the highly social and curious nature of budgies makes them wonderfully interactive pets. In our home, "John Lennon" is free-flying throughout the day and placed in his cage at night. He perches on a large houseplant to sing his distinctive morning and evening songs. He is very playful, and although he has his designated cache of toys, he incorporates a variety of other objects into his games.

Set-up costs: From $25 for a parakeet up to $100 for a cockatiel. Costs for the cage and other supplies vary from $50 to upwards of $5,000.

Monthly maintenance costs: $5 -$7.

Vet care: $$100 annually.

Daily time commitment: 20 minutes of basic daily care. At least 20 minutes a day for playtime, handling time, and interaction time.

Pets That Need the Most Care

Kittens and cats

Currently, more homes in the United States have felines than any other pet. They can easily live fourteen to seventeen years; some can live upwards of twenty. Because of cats' longevity, families should give careful deliberation to their lifestyle and housing arrangements before considering adoption. Cats and kittens are ideal pets for most children. They are tolerant of handling and will generally seek out interactions. They can be the best of companions during reading or homework times, curling up on a lap or beside the child on the bed.

Quick movements and loud noises can startle cats. If they are cornered and frightened, they will defend themselves with tooth and claw. This is normal behavior even if the defense is against the best intentions of a child. Therefore, it is important that children be taught how to read and respect the "leave me alone" signals of their feline companion. In addition, it is the parent's role to enforce the quiet time essential for the cat's mental health. Gentle, consistent, respectful handling from "kittenhood" through adulthood will ensure a wonderful companion cat.

Some people make the assumption that all cats are alike, but just like dogs, different breeds display distinct personalities. Learning about breed-associated traits can be helpful before you purchase or adopt a cat. It might be a good idea to attend a cat show. There you will be able to talk to different cat breeders and find out more about grooming requirements and behavioral traits of the cat you are considering.

Many people adopt cats from the animal shelter where the heart tends to rule the head. While most of the cats found there are not "blue bloods, " they will still carry characteristics of their ancestry. For instance, Siamese cats are renowned for their unique and aggressive vocalizations. If the yowl of an excited feline sets your hair on end, cats carrying Siamese characteristics should be off your list of potential adoptees.

Cats are playful, and their athletic antics make them very engaging. Like children, they tend to prefer the wrapper to the toy. This is great on the pocketbook, and the family can have fun creating cat toys. Some of their homemade favorites include paper rolled into a ball, paper bags, plastic rings from milk jugs, and wrapping paper.

Cats are lower maintenance than dogs or horses but require more regular care and attention than some of the smaller animals we have previously discussed. The belief that cats are aloof and therefore require little care is a myth. Cats need affection and will form a strong bond with their owner. Fresh food and clean water is required  daily; the litter box should be cleaned regularly since cats are fussy about their toilet. Cats must have yearly vet care for booster vaccines, and they should also be checked for worms. Like dogs, cats should also be spayed or neutered. Regular nail trimmings are recommended for indoor cats in addition to having a scratching post handy. All of the long haired breeds will also need regular grooming to keep their coat and skin healthy. Keep all of the care and health issues in mind while selecting your cat.

Because cats are so inquisitive, some household items can present hazards. Drapery and blind cords are irresistible to young cats but have the potential of becoming tangled around the animal. These should be wrapped up and out of the way of even the highest of leapers. Cats tend to lie in warm areas and places that form natural caves so check the insides of dryers and under recliners before operating them.

Cats like to eat grasses and will choose to munch on house-plants even though some are poisonous. Safe edibles, such as grasses and catnip, can be purchased through your local pet store or nursery. These will entice your cat, satisfy its desire for greens, and leave your houseplants intact.

There is a wide range of commercial foods available. I highly recommend choosing a premium quality, "human-grade" food. Although these cost a bit more, your cat will be healthier, and therefore, you will have less vet expense. According to Scott Price, a pet nutritionist, cats fed an optimal diet also live longer, lead more active lives, and in general, need fewer parasite controls than those fed commercial pet foods.

Although walks are not required, cats do need regular exer-cise to keep them in good physical condition and to reduce stress. Boredom, as with any animal, will lead to health problems and destructive behaviors. Cats love to play, and games are a great form of exercise, interaction, and just a jolly good time. Don't assume children know the proper way to play with kitty. Take the time to show them the ins and outs of feline etiquette. For example, to avoid scratches, teach children not to use their hands as toys.

Some families will allow their cat to venture out into the wilds of their back yard. Although some cats love the opportunity to com-mune with nature, not all cats like the great outdoors. Some may find the wide open too scary while other breeds, such as Persians, don't do well outside because of respiratory restrictions. There are some additional health issues that should be considered for the indoor/outdoor cat. Outdoor cats are more exposed to parasites both from fleas and from the food they get on their hunting for-ays. Therefore, more active parasite control should be maintained. Because cats are so athletic, they tend to disregard fences or other such boundaries and therefore may be subjected to injury from autos, dogs, and even other cats. Some feline behaviorists believe that cats should only be indoor animals and allowed outside only with careful supervision.

Contrary to popular belief, cats are trainable and can be taught house rules. Training time and sophistication depends on each family's preference. Should you be so inclined, cats can be taught such things as walking on a leash, coming when called, "sit" and "down" on command, "sit and stay" (for a short period of time), and traveling relaxed in a kennel. They can also be trained to accept grooming and to roll over. Whatever your household requires, a cat can be a welcomed addition.

Set up cost: $10 and up depending on where you adopt your cat and what goodies you purchase to go with it. There are a lot of extras available for the cat lover, but remember that all the pet needs is a clean, warm, safe spot to sleep, good food, fresh water, and lots of love. The rest are frills.

Monthly maintenance cost: $10 per bag for a good quality food $14 per bag for litter if the cat is kept solely indoors.

Vet care: Yearly vaccines, $ 35-$60; worming 25-35, one-time cost of altering, $50-100 to spay or neuter..

Daily time commitment: 10 to 20 minutes daily plus interaction time.

Dogs and puppies

Dogs are the second most popular of all the family pets. Wonderfully interactive, dogs offer as much love back to their family as they get from it. Dogs come in various shapes and sizes, personalities, and grooming and exercise requirements. One thing is certain, even with the variability, all dogs require a high level of commitment from their owners. Most dogs require much more interaction than the previously mentioned pets. In addition to the regular maintenance, there is grooming that includes not only brushing and trimming hair but also ear, eye, and teeth cleaning. It's beneficial, for both the child and the dog to keep a regular schedule for the dog's care. As with cats, feeding, providing clean water, and cleaning the living area must be done daily.

Depending on the dog, grooming may be a daily chore or one that is tackled on a weekly basis. Both the child and the dog can learn together through obedience lessons, feeding exercises and evening massage sessions. Massage should be a pleasant, relaxed, and calming activity for your dog. It is also educational. The dog learns to relax when touched, making it easier to medicate and to groom him. The child learns appropriate ways to touch and handle the dog and discovers the pet's favorite place to be stroked or scratched.

All dogs need schooling. The best program will be one that entails instruction for the parents, the child, and the dog. Interview the trainer before you enroll in a program. This way you are insured that the instructor is comfortable working with children and that the class will be appropriate both for the age of the child and for the dog. Locate classes that focus on positive reinforcement methods. These techniques will build a relationship between the pet and the child. I cannot stress enough the importance of regular training. Just like a child's schooling, training needs to be practiced at least five days a week for a period of fifteen to twenty minutes at a session.

Although dogs mature faster than human children, education should continue on a regular basis throughout the animal's life. Your dog may be proficient at basic obedience, but continuing the dog's education provides mental stimulation, very much as a job or schooling does for people. The continued training also enriches the bond between the dog and its teacher.

Most dog breeds have clubs that sponsor activities in which your child can participate. Many of the activities are designed to showcase the dog's natural talent. These arenas of competition can provide a great challenge for the dog/child team. Becoming involved in some of these activities will provide new training ideas, set attainable goals, and provide growth as the team strives for greater aspirations. It can also be a great social event for young people to meet others with similar interests.

-Erin McCune, Grade 1

Children do not naturally understand proper canine etiquette, so parents are responsible for the judicious treatment of the dog. The news regularly reports accidental dog bites inflicted on children. Many more incidents go unreported as the majority is from the beloved family pet. Most often these mishaps can be avoided. Children should never be allowed to sit on or crawl over the dog, even if it puts up with such treatment. Children should never be allowed to pull the ears or the tail or pinch lips or toes. The dog should have a safe place to go when family activity becomes overwhelming. It also needs a private place to enjoy food in peace and quiet.

Dogs, more than any other pet, are involved with the daily interactions of the family life. All of these opportunities promote a rich fodder from which life teachings can occur.

Set-up costs: $150 to $3,000, depending on where you adopt your dog and the type of dog.

Monthly maintenance costs: Around $35.00 per 40 lb. bag of high quality food. Good quality is important. In addition to the reasons given for cats, cleaning up the yard after your dog is much easier and less work with a high-grade food. The amount you will need to feed will depend on the size and metabolism of your dog. Be sure to watch your pet's weight carefully and go easy on the doggie treats. In America, both dog and cat obesity is epidemic.

Vet costs: Yearly vaccines, $50 to $150, depending on what is required for your area and local vet charges; worming medications, $25-50; spay, $150; neuter, $75. (These are approximate costs and may vary over different parts of the country. Please call a local veterinarian for accurate costs in your area.)

Daily time commitment: About 60 minutes for cleaning, exercising, and training plus interaction time. Dogs like companionship. Children can take advantage of this and read to the dog or do their homework by them. Don't forget the outdoor time. Children need physical exercise as much as their dogs.

Final Note

Living with a pet evokes deep feelings, and their eventual loss can impact the family as deeply as the loss of a human family member. It is the anticipation of this very painful experience that prevents some parents from allowing their lives to become entwined with that of a pet. But to deny our children this joyous experience because of the parent's fear of pain encourages a cautious approach to life. "It is far better to have loved and lost than never to have loved at all."

One day, our children will be faced with the death of a human they love. Birth, life, and death are the cycles of the natural world.

Small losses, such as a crushed flower or perhaps the death of a favorite fish, allow us to practice handling grief. Learning that grieving is a process, not a permanent condition, helps our children to understand that pain they feel will pass and that grief is a natural part of a balanced human psyche. Allowing our children to practice these processes while still enveloped in the safety of the family is an invaluable gift. The joyous risk of sharing our hearts is worth every tear that is shed. (For more on handling the death of a pet, see the chapter "Pets and the Circle of Life.")

Suggestions for Maximum Success for Pet Ownership

1) Study your pet's needs together as a family. Enlist the help of even the smallest member when planning the ins and outs of pet ownership.

2) Assign age appropriate chores. Remember that young children may have good intentions but they often forget all of the steps for a chore or they may not do a complete job. Older children and parents should coach and help them, but be respectful of the fact that the chore is theirs. Allow them to do the work and get the praise.

3) Define tasks clearly. State exactly when a job should be done, where it should be done, and how it should be done. Work together with children, performing the chore several times until you are just standing by and observing. After the child solos, be sure to follow up with periodic inspections to insure that the quality of the work is not slipping. Be careful about criticism. Instead, look for all of the things the child did right before you point out errors. By focusing on the positive, the child will grow and learn from the experience rather than feel defeated. If the job is not done correctly, back up and work with the child again.

(For more detail see the section, "Responsibility," in the chapter "The Role of a Pet in the Changing Child.")

Other Considerations before You Buy a Pet

How much time do you have? Busy families should consider a low maintenance pet. First-time pet parents should also consider this option. It is also important to consider the longevity of the pet you are considering. Family time restrictions change as the children in the family grow therefore when considering a pet with higher time demands, plan for the entire life of the pet.

Do you have other pets? Consider how existing family pets will accept this new addition to the family. If you have a bird that is used to flying free, getting an indoor cat may be a problem.

How much space do you have? Pets that require lots of space for exercise are not good choices for apartment dwellers.

Do you rent or own your home? If you are renting, consider what may happen if you have to move. Some rental contracts don't allow pets, even if your current one does.

Are you prepared for the costs of owning a pet? Consider carefully all of the associated costs of owning a pet, not just the purchase price. Are you prepared to pay vet expenses if the pet experiences an illness or injury? Take into account family vacations. You may go to places that will not permit the family pet to go, too. Are you prepared to hire a pet sitter or send your pet away to a boarding facility?

How much maintenance are you willing to take on? Have a family meeting and discuss all of the different tasks associated with the kind of pet you are considering adopting. Make sure that everyone is willing to give a little of his or her time for this new member of the family. You may want to draw up contracts for older family members and have them sign their commitment. Hold them to their promise.

NATURE IN THE LIVES OF CHILDREN

"To educate our people, and especially our children, to humane attitudes and actions toward living things is to preserve and strengthen our national heritage and the moral values we champion in the world."

- John F. Kennedy.

Families that, for whatever reason, choose not to have a pet can still reap the teaching benefits of animals by visiting them in their natural habitat. A city park can be a great introduction to nature and to the environment. Very young children are attuned to seeing what adults often miss. Little insects and plant life thrive in the cracks of sidewalks that are like tiny villages bustling with activity.

"When a child gets to know a tree in winter when it is covered with snow and adorned with icicles, the child will know the tree more thoroughly in the summer," said Arabella Buckley, children's author and naturalist. Speaking about the parent's role in educating children about nature she writes, "It is better that it should be an unconscious influence. If a parent feels it [enthusiasm for nature], rest assured the child will feel it. For children are much nearer to Nature than we who are older. The flowers, bees, and birds are far more part of their world than in the case of grown people whose minds have become clogged with the conventionalities of life. When eager questions are carefully answered, with a real desire to find out the purpose underlying all things, it is not only an education but also a great delight to them."

Children love adventure. Go on a quest. Touch trees, notice their textures, feel the weight of rocks. Identify as many different plants and animals as you can. If the plant, animal, or mineral is new, study the specimen as closely as possible, committing the details to memory so that you can identify it when you get home. Many animals such as a grasshopper, plant hopper, or ant can be studied from the palm of your hand. You don't need to know about everything; you just need to be willing to learn with your child. Do whatever captures the essence of this adventure.

Lots of my friends live here.
I held a bee on my finger once. Their feet are very tiny.
Ants can carry pieces of your cookie.
Grasshoppers tickle when you hold them.
I learned to jump with Swasoo, my grasshopper.
Wanna see?

- Margaret Hevel

Some areas of discovery, such as national parks, don't allow collecting. That's okay. Family explorers can draw pictures, take rubbings, write notes, compose poems, make up a song or dance, or tell a story. Don't be afraid to let your children see a vulnerable part of you. Listen with awe to the wisdom that comes from their innocence.

When you return from your outing, try sitting down with your child and writing for ten to fifteen minutes. Write whatever words or images leap from your pen onto the page. With younger children you can draw pictures or tell a story. When you and your child have finished, invite your child to share what he or she has written or tell a story about the drawing. Children are very interested in your view of the world. Let them know that their insights are no less valuable than yours. There is no right or wrong answer.

Don't be critical; this is no place to be concerned with punctuation or grammar. Listen, praise, and enjoy. By encouraging your children to share through your unconditional acceptance no matter what they are expressing, you are opening communication, helping them to know that you love and accept them for who they are, not who you wished they would be.

An empty dandelion stem. Make a wish before it hits the ground . . .
the fairy dust I blew . . .
Wanna see?

- Margaret Hevel

Charlotte Mason (1842-1923) was an English educator who understood the value of nature in a child's education. During a time when schools promoted "spare the rod and spoil the child" and the three "R's" of reading, writing and 'rithemtic, Mason encouraged parents to augment their children's education by exposing them to the wonders of nature.

The study of nature is entirely investigative. Questions arise naturally from observations of nature and of the environment. Why is this…? What happens when…? What if…? Answers may be provided by a simple trip to the library or by surfing the Web. A more dynamic way to answer a child's question, however, would be to design an experiment. This might include the fundamentals of all scientific research. For instance, you could begin by writing a hypothesis (what the child thinks is going to happen), then setting up your experiment (the methods), and detailing observations that you and your child make throughout the entire experiment. Remember to collect your data (the results) impartially. Finally, based on your observations, you and your child could draw a conclusion, pulling together all that you learned. Did the conclusion match the hypothesis? Why not? The process of asking questions, so natural for children, considering the options, and then drawing conclusions is the foundation for critical thinking.

"Nature walks, these are the great times of finding out. One must use them to point out leaf mosaic, plant association, bird song, habitats of plants, habits of growth, but they should also be regarded as times when the children seek for themselves and should be encouraged to go and observe by themselves."

- V.C. Curry

Visiting nature as the seasons change provides opportunities for children to experience cyclic rhythms. Breathe the fragrance of trees, grasses, and dirt. Can you tell the arrival of a new season by the scent that it carries? Spring in the Northwest smells damp and earthy and carries the scent of new life, like a baby awakening and exhaling warm sweet breath. Summer creeps in almost unnoticed while spring and fall changes are so pungent and clear that my children and I know the exact day the new season begins.

"At Easter, the tadpoles and newts in ponds, the nesting of birds, the early flowers and bird-song can all be studied. At Whitsuntide, flowers and insects, with their relation to each other, the life of bees, butterflies and ants, in fact the whole range of plant and animal life offer themselves for study. In Autumn, the flowers are nearly over but we have fruits and cereals, the habits of game animals, the flocking of birds before they migrate and by the seaside, life in the pools is very rich and abundant, while the short evenings bring the stars again in view."

- Arabella Buckley

Notice the light as it changes with the seasons. The color and texture of familiar objects transform as they pass through the season's hues, the brightness of summer, the blue-gray hue of winter. As one of my teachers used to say, "Notice what you notice."

Animal behavior also changes with the approach of a new season. Observe which animals stay through the winter, which ones leave the latest in the fall, and which appear first in the spring. Do some of the animals from your backyard hibernate? It might be fun to research what kinds of food your resident animals eat. You can encourage an animal to stay year round by changing food resources to match the season.

"The main thing, however, is to lead the children to see what is around them and to enter the life of all living beings. In this way they will learn to look upon nature as part of the one great scheme under which we all live, doing each our own work for the good of all as best we may; that by our efforts we may both improve ourselves and help others..."

-Arabella Buckley

As parents, we can teach respect for Nature and all forms of life. Stomping on insects is a learned behavior. Observe ants, talk about their hard work and their role in the ecosystem. With knowledge, respect naturally develops. Everything in the natural world has a purpose.

The alluring magic of nature can change the lives of children, forever transforming their view of the world. This gift cannot be purchased. Teaching the web of life by living and breathing it is more valuable than gaining it in any other fashion, including computer software, books, or television nature programs.

I run in the meadow and the wind runs with me.
Everyone is happy here.
The grass and flowers wave when I come out to play.
There's the pond. If you hold your breath like this . . .
And keep your eyes open like this . . .
You can see where the fish and turtles live in the pond.

Everything looks squiggly in the water.
Wanna see?

- Margaret Hevel

Tips for Sharing Nature with Your Children

Your attitude, sense of awe, reverence, and curiosity are much more important than your knowledge. Joseph Cornell, the author of *Sharing Nature with Children*, lists five commandments for outdoor education:

1) Teach less and share more. Don't be afraid to show your emotions. Experiencing nature paint the sky at sunset or orchestrating her symphony at sunrise is exciting.

2) Be receptive. Listen to the whisper of the leaves in the trees, to the trilling song of a male robin defending his territory or calling for a future mate. Be aware of the musty smell in the forest path that says mushrooms are near. Feel the change in temperature as you walk from sunlight to the shade of the forest. Become attuned to the sharp taste of pine in the air. Listen, look, and feel what your child does. Match his step, breath, and heartbeat.

3) Focus the child's attention without delay. As you encounter nature, pull your child[ren] into your experience, and then ask them to share theirs. Become a part of each other's world.

4) Look and experience first; talk later. Let your child feel the caterpillar's suction feet inch [its] way across his palm before you talk about the marvel of the insect's transformation. Select a moment to teach when there is a pause in nature's wonder.

5) A sense of joy should permeate the experience; enthusiasm is contagious. The long-lasting impression your child will take away from the experience should be one of awe and a desire to know more. A love and appreciation of nature is the most powerful gift that you can give.

Suggestions to Naturalize Your Outdoor Play Space

1) Plant native wildflowers. These will attract butterflies hungry for their nectar.

2) Create a natural area containing rock and log piles. Have toys available so children can use their imaginations in this natural setting. According to Maria Minno (Why Children Should Study Nature), "You don't need to plant anything, in fact, if you do you'll be missing out on one of the most interesting things; how seeds plant themselves!" She also suggests leaving a patch of grass un-mowed and watching the changes of nature's artistry.

3) Plant a vegetable garden.

4) Compost. Compost provides rich mulch for the lawn, flowerbeds, and garden. The process will also provide rich fodder for the discussion of microorganism and the most basic and important link in the food chain.

5) Keep bird feeders full year round. Also fill hummingbird and oriole feeders in the summer.

- Canadian Resource sheet #43

Children can be enlisted to help the world on a personal basis. Here are ten simple ways to protect our planetary home for people and all living creatures.

1) Use nontoxic products for household cleaning. Be aware of the packaging of products. Choose recyclable items over things that create more landfills.

2) Practice the three R's: reduce, recycle, and reuse.

3) Use items with the least environmental impact (reusable items verses disposable ones).

4) Conserve energy.

5) Use greener energy sources, such as solar or wind power, whenever possible.

6) Support companies that are environmentally conscious.

7) Eliminate the use of herbicides, pesticides, and other unnecessary toxins.

8) Support organizations that protect the environment.

9) Plant native trees, shrubs, and flowers.

10) Educate others how little, positive steps can make a huge difference. No one is expected to do everything, but everyone is expected to do something.

Because we touch, hold and physically investigate nature, we bond with it. Participating in the lives of animals helps to keep children connected to nature throughout their growing years. At a time when video games, computers, and television threatens to engulf our children, it is important for them to remain connected to the natural world for their future and for the future of all of humanity.

Pussywillows

Pussywillows, gray and gold plumage of spring
Decorating graceful stems of brown
Greetings.
Reflective moments recall
Childhood escapades hunting bullfrogs by the pond
Mud turtles, fifty-cent size, sunbathing on a log.
An iridescent butterfly darts and flits
Just beyond my reach.
Pausing by the pussy willow bush, I bend
We meet nose to nose.
Grinning with delight I sneeze
Blowing golden flower dust into the breeze.
Fairy sprinkles, I close my eyes and make a wish.
Pussy willows, gray and gold plumage of spring
Decorating stems of brown
Greetings.

- Margaret Hevel

SOME FINAL THOUGHTS

"If we put our problem solving abilities in high gear and join hands and brains and hearts around the world, surely we can find ways to live that are more in harmony with nature and start to heal some of the wounds we have inflicted. After all, humans have accomplished 'impossible' tasks before."

-Jane Goodall,
A Reason for Hope

According to Marion Diamond, a child's intelligence is directly tied to the richness of his or her environment. In other words, who we become as adults is dictated in part by the experiences we have between childhood and adulthood. This journey is not easy. Parents and children are faced with daily decisions on how to interact with and react to their environment. Children exposed to the emotional and practical experiences with a family pet will grow into whole, more well-rounded people than those without this awareness.

Pets augment the lessons we teach. Although they cannot take a parent's place in raising children, pets can help to remind parents that many of the things we find stressful, such as business meetings, traffic jams, frustrating coworkers, aren't really that important. Animals have a profound effect on human physiology. They slow the heart rate, lower blood pressure, and temper emotions. They remind us to laugh.

Pets facilitate social interactions. Children from pet-owning homes have better verbal and nonverbal communication skills than those from non-pet-owning families. Pets can help teens through awkward adolescence. They are a safe treasure from their childhood, something for them to cling to when it seems as if their world is falling apart. Interacting with a family pet, as in walking the family dog, reduces anxiety. A family pet can be a conduit for open positive communication between parent and child.

Pets give parents permission to be intuitive. There are myriad teaching and parenting tools to guide us, but ultimately what we, as parents, choose, is a matter of intuition. Sometimes we find it difficult to trust these "gut feelings," especially when we are trying to do the right thing regarding our children. We would rather rely on the words from experts to lead the way through this confusing maze. Pets are in tune with their instincts and can therefore be teachers to parents as well. Observing pets as they interact with our children can teach us powerful lessons. We can enlist their help when teaching a child to be compassionate. We can teach patience to our children by modeling how to control our anger and frustration. Pets immediately convey their needs and feelings. This basic communication teaches children in a way that is easy to understand. Children learn to be responsible for their behavior.

Pets help children gain self-confidence. Caring for pets leads to punctuality, tidiness, and self-discipline. Training a pet teaches patience, self-control, and delayed gratification. For most people, these skills don't come naturally. With a family pet, parents can help teach their child to control counter-productive impulses. Feelings of frustration and anger are natural but are not the fault of another person or a pet.

Pets provide a sense of security. Two working parents are the financial support for many families. Because of this, children may come home from school to an empty house. For children to learn to trust and to acquire self-confidence, they need to feel secure. A family pet provides a sense of security and companionship and helps a child learn how to productively spend time alone.

Pets teach responsibility. Providing for the needs of another helps children to understand that they are important and unique. What they do has impact on the well-being of another life. Fulfilling obligations fills up the child's integrity well. Promises that are kept to the pet (I will care for you), to themselves (I will be responsible), and ultimately to others, are invaluable for building self-worth. Assuming responsibility sets a behavioral pattern that has global reverberations.

Pets teach life lessons. Animals are in tune with the earth's natural rhythm. A child's first experiences with the miracle of birth and the finality of death often come from a family pet. As children understand how these natural processes connect to their own lives, they take a step toward becoming an adult.

Pets provide companionship. Raising children is a complex process and an ongoing challenge. As parents, we try to provide a foundation for our children. When our children grow and step out into an ever-changing world, a family pet can offer support during the transition from childhood to adulthood. For example, when a child is frustrated, the comfort of a pet can smooth the rough edges of his or her emotions. The nonjudgmental companionship of pets can provide a restorative balance for the whole family. Pets offer playfulness, a steady presence, and attention when it seems to be needed most.

Pets can enrich the relationship between parent and child. They can serve as a safe outlet for family members to share emotions and feelings that might not otherwise be discussed. Their calming presence and their delightful antics help bridge the gap between two very different worlds, childhood and adulthood. We encourage you to use this bridge and take a step toward your child's world. We invite you to experience the magic of raising children with animals!

REFERENCES

American Academy of Child and Adolescent Psychiatry, Children and Pets. 2003. www.familyresource.com/parenting/38/205/

American Society for the Prevention of Cruelty to Animals. Adoption Tips. 2005. www.aspca.org

American Society for the Prevention of Cruelty to Animals. Pets as Presents: Planning Makes all the Difference. 2005. www.aspca.org.

American Society for the Prevention of Cruelty to Animals. Pocket Change. Clearing up some of the Perceptions and Misconceptions about Small Pet Mammals. 2004. www.aspca.org.

Arambasic, L. PhD and G. Kerestes, M.A. Facility of Philosophy, Department of Psychology, 1000 Zagreb, Luciceva 3 Crotia. 1998. The Role of Pet Ownership as a Possible Buffer Variable in Traumatic Experience, Presented at the 8th International Conference on Human-Animal Interactions, The Changing Roles of Animals in Society, Prague, September 10-12, 1998

Ascione, Frank R., PhD Department of Psychology, Utah State University, Logan, Utah 84322, Enhancing Children's Attitudes about the Humane Treatment of Animals: Generalization to Human-Directed Empathy. Anthrozoos. 5(3). 1992.

Ascione, Frank R., PhD and Claudia V Weber, M.S. Department of Psychology, Utah State University, Logan, Utah 84322. Children's Attitudes about the Humane Treatment of Animals and Empathy: One-Year Follow up of a School-Based Intervention. Anthrozoos 9(4) .1996: 188-195.

Asher, S.R. and J.D. Coie (Eds) Peer Rejection in Childhood. Cambridge University Press. 1992.

Asher, S.R. and J. Cassidy. Loneliness and Peer Relations in Young Children. Child Development. 63(2). 1992: 350-365.

Bairey, Steph. How Much Does it Cost to Own a Pet? 2001. www.familyresource.com

Basrur, Namita. Pets and Kids. 2001. www.evesindia.com/family/pets/petsandchildren.html.

Becker, Dr. Marty. The Healing Power of Pets. Hyperion, New York. 2002.

Blue, Gladys F. The Value of Pets in Children's Lives. Childhood Education 63. 1986: 84-90.

Bodmer, NM, Institutes of Psychology, Univeristy of Berne, 3000 Beme 9, Switzerland..Effects of Pet Ownership on the Well-Being of Adolescents with Few Familial Resources. 7th International Conference on Human-Animal Interactions, Animals, Health and Quality of Life, Geneva Switzerland. September 6-9, 1995.

Brander, Donna. Prevention of Problems with Children and Dogs. 2007. www.petplanet.co.uk/petplanet/behaviour/behaviour_prevention.htm

Buckley, Miss Arabella. The Training of Children in the Observation of Nature. No. 455.2001. www.homeschooling-quest.com

Bulcroft, Kris, PhD. Pets in the American Family. People, Animals, Environment. 8(4) 1990:13-14.

Mavis Lewis-Webber. Canadian Child Care Federation. Exploring Nature with Children. Resource sheet #43. 2001. www.cfc-efc.ca/docs/cccf/rs043_en.htm

Checchi, Mary Jane. Are You the Right Pet For Me? New York, New York. St.Martin's Paperbacks.1999.

Chopra, Deepak. The Seven Spiritual Laws for Parents. New York, New York. Harmony Books.1997.

Christiansen, Bob. The Humane Community of America. Animals and Children. 2005. www.saveourstrays.com.

Coloroso, Barbara. Parenting Through Crisis. Harper Resource. 1994.

Cornell, Joseph B. Resources for Teaching and Sharing Nature. Texas Parks and Wildlife Education. www.tpwd.state.tx.us/edu/enved/resources.htm

Curry, VC. The Teaching of Nature Study. Parents review, 36(8) August 1925:529-537. www.homeschoolingquest.com.

Diamond, Marion PhD. and Janet Hopson. Magic Trees of the Mind. Plume Printing. 1999.

DeFranco, Robert. Human Animal Bond. Family Choices and Family Losses, a Need for Understanding. The Behavior Counselor. Fourth quarter, 2002. www.animalbehaviorcounselors.org/members/newsletter/1002/familychoices.shtml

DeGruy. Kids and Dogs: A Common Sense Approach. Dog Owners Guide. May 2002. www.canismajor.com

The Detroit News. Make owning pets a family affair. May 16, 2001. www.detnews.com/2001/homelife.

Dobson, Dr. James. Hide and Seek (How to Build Self-Esteem in Your Child). Fleming H. Revel Co. 1971.

Dyer, W.W. What Do You Really Want From Your Children? Avon Books. 1997.

Emsiwiler, Mary Ann and James Emsiwiler. Guiding Your Child Through Grief. Bantum Books. 2000.

Endenburg, Nieke and Ben Baarda. The Role of Pets in Enhancing Human Well-Being: Effects on Child Development. Reprinted from Waltham Book of Human-Animal Interactions: Benefits and Responsibilities. Courtesy of Waltham.

Faber, Adele and Elaine Mazlish. How to Talk so Kids will Listen and Listen so Kids will Talk. Avon Books. 1999.

Faber, Adele and Elaine Mazliah. Siblings without Rivalry. Avon Books. 1987.

Faber, Adele and Elaine Mazlish. Liberated Parents/Liberated Children. Avon Books. 1990.

Faber, Adele and Elaine Mazlish. Together. Avon Books. 1998.

Faull, Jan. Answering a Child's Questions about Death. Child Development and Behavior Specialist. www.familyfun. go.com.

Feldt, Gloria. All About Sex: A Family Resource on Sex and Sexuality. Planned Parenthood Federation of America. Three Rivers Press. 2003.

Fitzgerald, Helen. The Grieving Teen: A Guide for Teenagers and their Friends. Fireside Publishers. 2000.

Gandini, L., C. Edwards and G. Forman. The Hundred Languages of Children. Alblex.Ed 355-034 Norwood, New Jersey. 1993. www.eric.ed.gov.

Ginott, Haim M.D. Between Parent and Child. Three Rivers Press. 2003.

Gladding, Samuel T. Family Therapy: History, Theory and Practice. Prentice Hall. 2001.

Goldman, Daniel. Emotional Intelligence. Why it Can Matter More Than I.Q. Bantam Books. New York, NewYork. 1995.

Goodall, Jane and Marc Bekoff. The Ten Trusts. What We Must Do To Care For The Animals We Love. Harper Collins. San Francisco. 2002.

Gordon, Dr. Thomas. P.E.T. (Parent Effective Training).Peter H. Wyden Inc. 1970.

Gordon, Dr. Thomas. Discipline that Works. Plume Printing. 1991.

Green, Gina. Kid's best friends: Pets help prevent Allergies. August 28, 2002. www.cnn.health.com

Harris, Aubrey. Why Did He Die? Lerner Publishing Co. 1965.

Hendrich, Nichole, BA, RVT. The Human Animal Bond "Why We Love Animals. Society of Veterinary Behavior Technicians. 2002. www.svbt.org/articles/why_we_love_animals.html.

Henry, Shari. Homeschooling, the Middle Years. Puma Publishing. 1999.

Hubert, Cynthia. Creature Comfort. The Sacramento Bee, Tuesday August 13,2002. www.sacbee.com/content/life-style/story/3963841p-4989320c.html.

Hunthausen, Wayne, DVM. Kids and Dogs-Avoiding Bite Problems. 1996. www.westwoodanimalhospital.com

Jenkins, Harvey. The Humans Side of Human Beings. Rational Island Publishers. 1994.

Jones, Alanna and A.E. Jones. 104 Activities that Build: self-esteem, teamwork, communication, anger management, self-discovery, and coping skills. Rec Room Publishing. 1998.

Karp, Harvey M.D. and Paula Spencer. The Happiest Toddler on the Block (one to four years old). Bantum Books. 2004.

Kubler-Ross, Elizabeth. On Death and Dying. Scribner. 1997.

Kubler-Ross, Elizabeth. Life Lessons. Scribner. 2001.

McDaniel, Jack and Colleen. Pooches and Small Fry. Parenting Skills for Dogs (and kids!). Doral Publishing, Inc. Wilsonville, Oregon. 1995.

McNichols, J.and GM Collis. Department of Psychology, University of Warwick, Coventry, West Midlands, Cv2 7AL, UK. Relationships Between Young People with Autism and their Pets. 7th International Conference on Human-Animal Interactions, Animals, Health and Quality of Life. Geneva Switzerland. September 6-9, 1995.

Melson, G.F. PhD, Professor. Department of Child Development and Family Studies, Purdue University. The Role of Companion Animals in Human Development. 7th International Conference on Human-Animal Interactions, Animals, Health and Quality of Life. Geneva Switzerland. September 6-9, 1995.

Melson, Gail F., PhD. Fostering Inter-Connectedness with Animals and Nature: The Developmental Benefits for Children. People, Animals, Environment. Fall 1990: 15-17.

Melson, Gail F., PhD, Alan Beck, ScD. Rona Schwartz, MS. Purdue State University, West Lafayette, IN 47907 Pets as Sources of Support for Mothers, Fathers and Young Children. 8th International Conference on Human-Animal Interactions; The Changing Roles of Animals in Society. Prague. September 10-12, 1998.

Minno, Maria. Why Children Should Study Nature. The Palmetto. Vol. 12(3) 1992.

Mundy, Michaelene. Sad isn't Bad. Abbey Press. 1998.

Nelson, Jane. EdD. Positive Discipline for Teenagers: Empowering your Teens and Yourself Through Kind and Firm Parenting. Prima Lifestyles. 2000.

Northeast Indiana Parent. Pets Can Teach Kids Responsibility. Kendallville Publishing. Winter 2001. www.kpcnews. net/special-sections/parent/parent3.html

O' Sullivan, Michael, editor. Humane Society of Canada. The Healing Power of Pets. April 10, 2003. www.humanesociety.com

O' Sullivan, Michael, editor. Humane Society of Canada. Add A Feline Fur Face to Your Family Asks the Humane Society of Canada (HSC). May 23, 2003. www.humanesociety.com

O' Sullivan, Michael, editor. Humane Society of Canada. A Better World Begins With a Single Act of Kindness to Animals Says the Humane Society of Canada (HSC). April 11, 2003. www.humanesociety.com

O' Sullivan, Michael, editor. Humane Society of Canada. New Years Resolution for a Healthier Planet. December 27, 2002. www.humanesociety.com

O' Sullivan, Michael, editor. Humane Society of Canada. Helping Elderly and their Pets can Reduce Health Care Costs Says the Humane Society of Canada.(HSC) October 13, 2002. www.humanesociety.com

O' Sullivan, Michael, editor. Humane Society of Canada. How Many Days Before Another Child is Bitten by a Dog? March 1, 2001. www.humanesociety.com.

Page Wise. Children and Pets: Forming Healthy Relationships. 2001. www.avsands.com

Poresky, Robert H., PhD Associate Professor, Family Studies and Human Services, Kansas State University, 312 Justin Hall, Manhattan, Kansas 66506.Companion Animals and Other Factors Affecting Young Children's Development. Anthrozoos. 9(4) 1996:159-168.

Rimm, Sylvia B. PhD. How to Parent so Children will Learn. Apple Publisher. 1990.

Salomon, A. PhD, Department of Psychology, Universite de Montreal, Montreal, P.Q. H3C 3J7.Animals as Means of Emotional Support and Companionship for Children Aged 9-13 Years Old. 7th International Conference on Human-Animal Interactions, Animals, Health and Quality of Life, Geneva Switzerland. September 6-9, 1995.

Schaefer, Charles PhD. And Teresa DiGeronimo M. (eds). How to Talk to Teens about Real Important Things. Jossey-Boss Publishers. 1999.

Schoen, Allen DVM. Kindred Spirits. How the Remarkable Bond Between Humans and Animals Can Change the Way we Live. Broadway books, New York. 2002.

Shelvo, S.P. Caring for your Baby and Young Child from Birth to Age Five. Bantam Books. 1998.

Siegler, Ava L. PhD. The Essential Guide to the New Adolescence. Plume Printing. 1998.

Steinberg, Laurene. You and Your Adolescent. (Parents Guide for Ages 10-20). Harper Resource. 1997.

Toeplitz, Zuzanna. PhD, Anna Matczak PhD, Anna Pitrowska PhD, Aleksandra Zygier . University of Warsaw. Warsaw Poland. Impact of Keeping Pets at Home Upon the Social Development of Children. 7th International Conference on Human-Animal Interactions, Animals, Health and Quality of Life. Geneva Switzerland. September 6-9, 1995.

Triebenbacher , SL, PhD East Carolina University, Greenville, NC; CC Wilson, PhD and G Fuller, MD, Uniformed Services University of Health Sciences, Bethesda, MD. The Relationship Between Companion Animals, Caregivers, and Family Functioning. 8th International Conference on Human-Animal Interactions, The Changing Roles of Animals in Society. Prague. September 10-12,1998.

Triebenbacher , SL, PhD East Carolina University, Greenville, NC. The Relationship between Attachment to Companion Animals and Self-Concept: A Developmental Perspective. 7th International Conference on Human-Animal Interactions, Health and Quality of Life. Geneva Switzerland. September 6, 1995..

Vickers, Jamie. Choose Proper Pets to Join the Family. Mississippi State University. www.msucares.com.

Vidovic, Vlasta Vizek, Vesna Vlahovic and Denis Bratka. Pet Ownership, Type and Socio-emotional Development of School Children. Anthrozoos. 12(4) 1999:211-217.

Wattleton, Faye and Elixabeth Keiffer. How to Talk to Your Child about Sexuality. Planned Parenthood. Doubleday and Company. 1986

Watts, Richard G. Straight Talk About Death with Young People. Westminster John Knox Press. 1975.

W-3 Commerce. Care for Turtles, Pet Mice and Pet Fish: Teach your Children Responsibility and Perseverance. 2002. www.small-house-pets.com

Zimmerman, Dr Matt. Pets and Children. Feiner and Associates. 2291 N. University Drive, Pembroke Pines, Fl. (954)962-3855.

http://www.tcsn.net/honeyspots/children2.htm 2003.

HELPFUL RESOURCES

Choosing a Pet

Complete Pet Owner Manuals   1-800-645-3476.

Booklets

The Delta Society. www.deltasociety.org for a variety of articles on the human-animal bond

www.ourbrisbane.com/living/pets for choosing a pet

www.petplanet.co.uk for information for children on small animals

Puppies USA   1-800-426-2516 offers booklets with helpful information

Humane Society of America. www.hsus.org.

Humane Society of Canada. www.humanesociety.com

Death and Grief

About Dying-an open family book for parents and children together. by Sara BonnetStein Walker and Co. 1983 Ne York, New York

Explaining Death to Children by Earl A. Grollman Beacon Press 1969 Boston

The Fall of Freddie the Leaf by Leo Buscaglia, PhD, Slack, 2002, New Jersey. An excellent book for young children.

On Death and Dying by Elisabeth Kubler-Ross. Scribner. 1997. Long Beach, CA

Straight Talk about Death with Young People by Richard G. Watts. Westminster John Knox Press. 1975. Louisville

Why Did He Die? by A. Harris and S. Dalky. Lerner Publishing Co.1974. Minneapolis, Mn.

Helpful websites:
www.griefnet.org
www.compassionbooks.com
www.elisabethkublerross.com

Raising Children

The American Academy of Child & Adolescent Psychiatry. Pets and Children (For Public Information: 1-800-333-7636)

www.family.go.com/rasingkids/child/dev/expert. Great Website for child/adult communication. Has articles such as "How to Listen to Your Kids," "Diversity & Acceptance," "Loving Your Child," " Real Communication with Your Adolescent." and "Age-Specific Guide: What to Tell Them & When (Healthy Sexuality.."

Parent Guides are available through the National School Public Relations Association, 1801 North Moore Street, Arlington, Virginia 22209.

Parenting Information: www.rollercoaster.com

For articles such as " A Parent's Checklist for Day Care," write to: U.S. Department of Health and Human Services Superintendent of Documents, U.S. Government Printing Office, Washington, D.C. 20402

Service and Therapy Dogs

R.E.A.D. (Reading Education Assistance Dogs) This excellent and innovative program was founded by Sandi Martin and implemented in the Salt Lake City Public Library in 1999. It can be found in many Public Libraries nationwide.

www.canineassistants.org

www.caninecompanions.org

www.tdi-dog.org

www.vet.purdue.edu   Center for the Human-Animal Bond

www.deltasociety.org   Human-Animal Health Connection

Training Dogs / Dogs and Children

www.dogsensecentral.com..Website for training your dog with free trainer advice

www.apdt.com Dog Training Association

www.iaabc.com Animal behavior counselors

www.dogsandstorks.com Great site for families expecting a child. Wonderful tips for introducing dog and baby.

Cat help and questions

catbehaviorassociates.com

www.iaabc.org

Any book written by Pam Johnson-Bennett

Bird help and questions

www3.upatsix.com/liz

www.iaabc.org

I A A B C

The International Association of Animal Behavior Consultants, Inc. is a professional association for the field of animal behavior consulting. The association represents the professional interests of behavior consultants throughout the world. It is involved with the problems, needs and changing patterns of animal-owner relationships, and helps to ensure that trained practitioners meet the public's needs. The association provides the tools and resources animal behavior professionals need to succeed. It works tirelessly to nourish the animal-human bond.

The association's members meet standards for education and training and are held to the highest ethical standards of the profession. Certified members qualify as Certified Animal Behavior Consultants (CABC). They work with multiple species, including dogs, cats, horses, birds and other animals. Associate members are consultants in practice, on the path to Certified membership.

The IAABC facilitates research, theory development and education. It develops standards for education and training, professional ethics, and the work of animal behavior consulting. The IAABC publishes a scholarly Journal and develops brochures that inform the public about the field of animal behavior consulting

www.iaabc.org

Dogs&Storks™ was created from the observation that too often families give up their dog once children are in the immediate future. What we discovered is that in the vast majority of cases, giving up the K9 "baby" was not necessary. What's missing is the information and resources parents need to handle and address the natural concerns and questions that they experience. We listened and created this specialized program to address the consistent questions and concerns hundreds of families have shared with us over the years in our Dog behavior consulting business.

Since the beginning of Dogs&Storks™ in 2002, we have discovered that many Grandparents, other extended family and childcare providers have questions they need answers to as well. Dogs&Storks™ invites all family and childcare providers to attend our program with the new parents at no extra fee. Dogs are all around us in the community and the more you know the better choices you can make with a child when encountering dogs.

In short, Dogs&Storks™ is about helping families set themselves up for success. Education is the key. By learning about your dog and how he communicates, your family can increase the safety of your kids, provide a life-long home for your companion and have fun too!

www.dogsandstorks.com

Appendix

Weekly Chore Chart for Daisy

Day of the week	Feed and water	Clean kennel	Train and playtime	Walks and playtime	Brush and clean teeth
Monday					
Tuesday					
Wednesday					
Thursday					
Friday					
Saturday					
Sunday					

ABOUT THE AUTHORS

Chris Hamer and Peg Hevel are parents as well as professionals in their own fields. Both authors have experienced first hand the attributes of animals as part of the family. They also share the special bond of being mother and daughter.

Peg Hevel, R.N., B.S.N., P.H.N, worked as a Nurse Health Educator, community/family liaison and family counselor in the Montana public school system. During that time, she counseled parents, students and staff on growth and development and communication, child abuse prevention and health related issues. She worked on local, state, national and international levels for Child Abuse and Neglect Prevention.

Peg has facilitated workshops and has presented at several national conferences including the National Conference on Child Abuse by the Humane Association. She was invited to present at the International Congress on Child Abuse/Neglect.

Peg was a consultant and reviewer of educational materials for Marsh Films, Kendall School for the Deaf and Gallandet College. She was a NARAH certified instructor with Whitewater Therapeutic Riding and Recreation Association in Salmon, Idaho.

Currently, Peg is a freelance author publishing articles in newspapers and magazines. She has also published stories in the books *Horses Tale for the Soul* series, Volume IV and V, *Dog Tales for the Soul, Changing Course, Happy Endings,* and *Chicken Soup for the Dog Lover's Soul* and a full length novel called, *The Ivory Elephant.*

Chris Hamer, M.S., Certified Canine Behavior Consultant, (CCBC) has worked with dogs and their families to develop better relationships for over twenty-five years. After getting her Master's degree in Animal Behavior from Western Washington University in 1985, Chris began professionally training gun dogs and was one of the first women to train gun dogs, including hunting retrievers, pointers, and flushers. She actively competed in AKC and NARHA hunt tests and is a qualified judge for all levels of the hunt test program. From 1983-1997, Chris owned and operated Wyndhaven Kennels in Northwest Washington State where she would oversee the training of over 50 dogs each day. She is the creator of Dog-Sense Seminars; a two-day intensive training designed to turn dog owners into their dog's leader and teacher.

Currently, Chris conducts family trainings intended to improve the relationships between families and their pets. She also gives private and in-home training and gun dog classes. She is a member of the American Pet Dog Trainer Association (APDT), a certified member and member of the board of directors of the International Association of Dog Behavior Counselors (IADBC) and the chairperson for the IADBC Education Collaborative.

Chris is the author of DogSense, Building a Bond through Obedience Training and a contributing author of Dog Tales for the Soul. She is a regular contributor for the nationally syndicated radio broadcast, Pet Tales. Chris lives in Mount Vernon Washington with two teenage boys, twelve laying hens, three dogs, two geese, a cat, a duck, two horses, and her husband of twenty-five years.

The authors can be reached at www.dogsensecentral.com and mchevel1@yahoo.com